FASCINATING FOOD

FOOD
AND CULTURE

BY ALEXIS BURLING

Essential Library
An Imprint of Abdo Publishing
abdobooks.com

ABDOBOOKS.COM

Published by Abdo Publishing, a division of ABDO, PO Box 398166, Minneapolis, Minnesota 55439. Copyright © 2025 by Abdo Consulting Group, Inc. International copyrights reserved in all countries. No part of this book may be reproduced in any form without written permission from the publisher. Essential Library™ is a trademark and logo of Abdo Publishing.

Printed in China.
102024
012025

THIS BOOK CONTAINS RECYCLED MATERIALS

Cover Photo: Shutterstock Images
Interior Photos: Shutterstock Images, 1, 8, 11, 15, 18, 42, 61 (animals), 65, 67, 68–69, 75, 93, 94; Joe Gough/Shutterstock Images, 5; iStockphoto, 12, 27, 30, 89; Mike Dotta/Shutterstock Images, 21; Kirsten Walla/iStockphoto, 23; Teri Virbickis/Shutterstock Images, 29; Mark Zhu/iStockphoto, 32; Mohammad Batmanglij/Mage Publishers, 35; Anna Ewa Bieniek/Shutterstock Images, 37; Godong/Universal Images Group/Getty Images, 41; Jong-Hyun Kim/Anadolu Agency/Getty Images, 46–47; Daria Kulkova/iStockphoto, 53; John Vachon/Library of Congress, 54; Sonja Filitz/Shutterstock Images, 56; Ilene Perlman/Shutterstock Images, 60; Red Line Editorial, 61 (graph); Kim Bensing Studio/Shutterstock Images, 72; Dima Skorina/Shutterstock Images, 79; Natalia Lisovskaya/Shutterstock Images, 80; Eduard Zhukov/Shutterstock Images, 83; Justin Sullivan/Getty Images News/Getty Images, 84; Pande Putu Hadi Wiguna/Shutterstock Images, 97

Editor: Kari Cornell
Series Designer: Maggie Villaume

Library of Congress Control Number: 2024938295

PUBLISHER'S CATALOGING-IN-PUBLICATION DATA

Names: Burling, Alexis, author.
Title: Food and culture / by Alexis Burling
Description: Minneapolis, Minnesota: ABDO Publishing, 2025 | Series: Fascinating food | Includes online resources and index.
Identifiers: ISBN 9781098295257 (lib. bdg.) | ISBN 9798384916253 (ebook)
Subjects: LCSH: Ethnic food--Juvenile literature. | Food customs--Juvenile literature. | Food habits--Juvenile literature. | Food preferences--Juvenile literature. | Food--Religious aspects--Juvenile literature.
Classification: DDC 394.12--dc23

CONTENTS

CHAPTER ONE
A CULINARY ADVENTURE................... 4

CHAPTER TWO
GLOBAL CUISINE 14

CHAPTER THREE
THE GLOBALIZATION OF FOOD 26

CHAPTER FOUR
FOOD AND FAITH 40

CHAPTER FIVE
ETHICAL DIETARY CHOICES 52

CHAPTER SIX
FARM TO TABLE.............................. 66

CHAPTER SEVEN
THE DINING EXPERIENCE 78

CHAPTER EIGHT
THE FUTURE OF FOOD CULTURE..... 88

ESSENTIAL FACTS 100
GLOSSARY 102
ADDITIONAL RESOURCES 104
SOURCE NOTES......................... 106
INDEX 110
ABOUT THE AUTHOR 112

CHAPTER ONE

A CULINARY ADVENTURE

Ever since he was a young boy, Waqar Abidi had been obsessed with trying new and unusual types of food and culinary experiences. Some kids in his class liked only foods such as pizza, chicken nuggets, and spaghetti. But Waqar preferred to be as adventurous as possible when it came to eating.

Waqar's open-mindedness toward food had a lot to do with his upbringing. His grandparents were from Lahore, Pakistan. Every time Waqar and his brother and parents left Chicago, Illinois, to visit them, they were treated to a gigantic feast to celebrate their arrival. All the relatives were invited, including his uncles, aunts, and 16 cousins.

Though Waqar loved playing soccer in the park or exploring the Lahore streets with his older cousins, his favorite thing to do was to spend time in the kitchen, watching Nani—his grandmother—cook.

Pakoras, naan, and savory stews are staples on a Pakistani table.

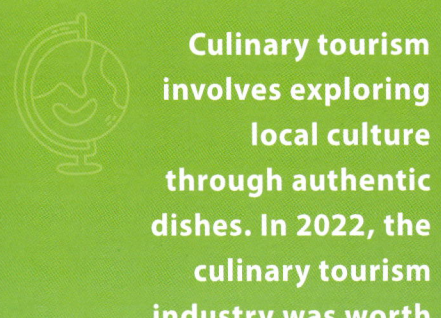

Culinary tourism involves exploring local culture through authentic dishes. In 2022, the culinary tourism industry was worth $804.95 billion.[1]

Nani was a genius in the kitchen. She made everything from scratch and entirely from memory, using whatever foods she had in the pantry. From mouth-watering appetizers to delectable desserts, there was nothing she couldn't whip up by hand. Over the years, Nani had introduced Waqar to some of the most thrilling flavors and textures he had ever encountered.

Because preparing meals is such an important part of Pakistani culture, Nani even taught Waqar how to make some of the dishes. Waqar loved helping her slice vegetables, roll them in a seasoned gram flour batter, and fry them to a crackling crisp to make finger-food snacks called pakoras. Waqar also enjoyed the strange, bitter taste of karela, a type of gourd known as bitter melon. The melon was bright green and had an oblong shape, so Waqar's brother sometimes threw it around the kitchen before Nani could grab it. Nani chopped the karela into cubes. Then she sautéed it with onions, red chili powder, turmeric, salt, coriander powder, and a pinch of cumin seeds to make a side dish that she served with rice.

Nothing got Waqar's stomach growling like watching Nani prepare a massive bowl of zarda as a dessert for the whole family. Made with basmati rice, sugar, milk, pistachios or almonds, and cardamom seeds, it was the perfect ending to a celebratory meal. Waqar especially loved that Nani didn't use artificial food coloring to give the rice its signature yellow color like some cooks did. Instead she used saffron, an expensive spice that she kept in her cupboard for this type of occasion.

But today, Waqar wasn't helping Nani prepare an eight-course meal. Instead of traveling to Pakistan for spring break, the Abidis decided to save up and take Waqar and his brother to Thailand for the first time. After spending nearly a day in different airports and on two planes, the family finally arrived in Bangkok, the capital of Thailand. Waqar was

A FESTIVE MULTINATIONAL TRADITION

In Pakistan, zarda is a festive treat often served at weddings and holiday gatherings. The dessert gets its name from the Urdu and Persian word *zard*, which means "yellow." But zarda isn't just a Pakistani treat. In fact, variations of the dessert are also served in other Muslim countries. In Iran, it's often made with butter. In India, cooks add ghee, which is clarified butter, plus cashews, raisins, coconut, and cloves. They call the dish *meethe chawal*. In Turkey, zarda was served at birth celebrations at the Ottoman Topkapi Palace in the 1500s.

already thinking about the food. He loved the Thai dishes he had tried in Chicago, such as pad thai, which is stir-fried rice noodles with pork, vegetables, and roasted peanuts. He also enjoyed tom yum goong, a clear broth made with lemongrass, mushrooms, shallots, lime juice, red chili peppers, shrimp, and fish sauce. He couldn't wait to experience more of the country's culinary traditions.

Zarda is a dessert made of sweet rice that is popular throughout the Indian subcontinent.

SPRING BREAK IN THAILAND

The culinary scene in Bangkok was everything Waqar had dreamed of and more. For the next week, the Abidis spent hours wandering around some of the city's famous night markets. The markets were filled with street-food vendors and small rooms lined with rickety stalls stacked high with clothing, housewares, produce, and meats. They enjoyed a meal at Baan Tepa, where diners can eat with the chef.

They also toured the restaurant's vast garden, where fresh ingredients on the menu grew. The family even tried 100 Mahaseth, a "nose-to-tail" restaurant that specializes in

Thai-raised beef, where every part of the cow that is edible is prepared to be consumed. Though Waqar and his brother were too afraid to try the dry-aged beef tongue, they did nibble on their dad's tripe crisps, made from the lining of a cow's stomach. Waqar thought they tasted like potato chips.

The Abidis loved all the food they tried in Bangkok. But in Waqar's mind, the best event was yet to come. That morning, he and his family had taken a ferry to Koh Kood, Thailand's fourth-largest but least-populated island. Waqar thought the beaches on Koh Kood were gorgeous—covered in fine golden sand and looking out over crystalline blue water. He couldn't get enough of strolling along the beach, looking out at the Gulf of Thailand, and drinking refreshing coconut water out of a real

FLOATING MARKETS

Bangkok is home to many types of markets, including floating markets. Before the city's roads were built in the early to mid-1900s, people traveled by boat using canals. Markets full of vendors in boats were packed with fruits, vegetables, seafood, and meats for sale. Today, most of Bangkok's floating markets cater to tourists. Taling Chan, one of the most popular, is located 7.5 miles (12 km) from downtown Bangkok.[2] There, vendors barbecue seafood on small grills and prepare papaya salad for diners seated at low tables near the water's edge. A larger local produce market helps provide an experience that is the best of both worlds.

coconut shell. But he was getting restless. He was so excited about the family's dinner plans at the Soneva Kiri resort that all he could think about was the meal he was about to experience—dinner in a bamboo pod high in the treetops.

A MEAL TO REMEMBER

When Waqar and his family arrived at Soneva Kiri, they were very hungry. After a short hike through the rainforest, they were greeted by one of the restaurant's hosts, who guided the family up a series of winding stairways. As they climbed, they listened to the rustle of 100-year-old Singapore almond trees and the melodious songs of Asian golden weaver birds in the background.

The guide then escorted the group to a bamboo pod the size of a dinner table. As soon as Waqar and his family were comfortably seated on their cushions with their seatbelts fastened, the guide pulled a giant lever. The pod rose slowly into the air on steel cables. By the time it stopped, the Abidis were looking out over the gulf from 36 feet (11 m) up as their pod swayed gently in the breeze.[3]

From start to finish, the family's hour-long meal at Soneva Kiri was worth every penny—at least in Waqar's mind. They dined on yellow and green mangoes,

A vendor at a floating market in Thailand prepares traditional noodle soups for customers.

mangosteen, and lychee from the resort's organic garden, fish and other seafood caught that morning, and a basket of sweet desserts. The most thrilling part of the experience was that the waiter delivered their food and drinks by zipline while strapped into a safety harness. He carried everything in baskets that hung from his arm. Waqar knew the treetop dining adventure wasn't a traditional part of Thai food culture, like some of the other dining options the Abidis had tried on their trip. Still, for him it felt like a once-in-a-lifetime experience—one he couldn't wait to tell Nani about during their next cook-off in her kitchen.

FASCINATING FOOD

For Waqar, food serves many purposes. Nutritious meals keep him healthy and strong. New food experiences make him happy. And cooking and dining are a way for him to connect to his heritage and learn about other cultures around the world. His culinary journeys at home and abroad are shaped by traditions passed down through generations. The foods he enjoys reflect centuries of history, migrations, cultural exchange, and other forces.

Diners enjoy an evening meal suspended above the beach on the island of Koh Kood, Thailand.

For many people all over the world, food is much more than what they eat to survive each day. Instead, it's closely tied to the culture in which they live. Some people, such as Orthodox Jews or Muslims, make dietary choices based on religious beliefs and prohibitions. Others, such as vegetarians or vegans, choose to eat a certain way because of their ethical beliefs or social values. No matter what foods people choose to eat, the experience of eating, whether it's a meal or snack, can be very personal. This experience can change throughout a person's lifetime.

Whether they're located in the United States or anywhere else in the world, many people believe that dining is best when enjoyed with friends and family. Some love to splurge on a high-end tasting menu that lasts for hours. Others prefer a home-cooked meal or a quick snack at a food truck. Wherever the destination and whatever the experience, a range of culinary traditions is available to satisfy every palate.

FISH FOR THE FEASTING

All across the United States, foods such as pad thai and pad woon sen have made their way onto menus as typical Thai cuisine. But on Thailand's many islands, some of the most popular dishes are made with locally grown herbs and fish because of the easy access. Pla kapong neung manao is sea bass steamed and served in a lime juice broth and then topped with garlic, cilantro, and diced chili peppers. Many Thai restaurants serve fish whole because it's meant to be shared with family and friends.

CHAPTER TWO

GLOBAL CUISINE

Food is what sustains all living things. Without the vitamins, nutrients, fats, and calories in food, people wouldn't have the energy to move, think, talk, or even breathe. But beyond keeping humans alive, food reflects social class and regional differences. Food is also a symbol of humanity's deep connection to history, culture, and national pride.

Around the world, hundreds of different types of regional and local cuisines link to as many cultures. Each cuisine tells a story of its people, their unique traditions, and even how they like to spend time with family and friends. These are just a sampling of the regional and national cuisines available to an adventurous eater in the world today.

Traditional Chinese soups combine flavorful broth, vegetables, and tofu or meat such as chicken, duck, or fish. Each region has its own signature recipes.

ASIAN CUISINE

In most cultures, the foods people eat depend on what natural resources, such as plants and animals, are accessible locally. China's recorded gastronomic history is more than 2,000 years old. Many ingredients, such as soybeans, rice, duck, and garlic, are common in various Chinese dishes, but they are often prepared differently depending on the region.

Chinese cooking has four major styles. The northern part of the country is home to the nation's political center. Its Lu (Shandong) cuisine is known for bold-flavored soups and dishes featuring locally caught seafood. In the western area, humid temperatures dictate which crops can be grown, and locals prefer more flavorful food. Here, spicy Chuan (Szechuan) cuisine such as diced chicken with peanuts and vegetables makes frequent use of the Szechuan peppercorn.

KIMCHI: A CULTURAL KOREAN ICON

For thousands of years, entire Korean villages have gathered to turn hundreds of heads of cabbage and piles of ginger and radishes into spicy fermented kimchi. As part of a tradition called kimjang, this was a time for women to trade gossip and discuss the news of the day. Kimjang is still an essential part of Korean culture. People there produce hundreds of varieties of kimchi. Around 1.5 million short tons (1.4 million metric tons) of it is eaten in South Korea each year.[1]

In the southern Guangdong Province, long an epicenter for foreign trade, crispy and delicately flavored Yue (Cantonese) cuisine uses steel pots called woks to create dishes such as stir-fried shrimp and mushrooms with oyster sauce. Su (Huaiyang) cuisine comes from the Jiangsu region in East China, known as the land of fish and rice. Famous dishes here include sweet-and-sour mandarin fish and boiled salted duck.

In Korea, communal eating—often between multiple generations—is a cherished tradition. Most meals consist of one main dish, such as Korean barbecue or beef bibimbap, that is shared among everyone at the table. For side items, Koreans serve a variety of smaller dishes before the main course, including pickled squid, a fermented cabbage mixture called kimchi, bean sprout salad, and scallion pancakes. Known as banchan, these small plates are meant to be eaten as appetizers and throughout the main meal to complement spicy and savory Korean flavors.

For centuries, fish has been a staple of the Japanese diet. As a nation made up of islands and streams, the country has easy access to saltwater and freshwater fish. Japanese people enjoy eating fish raw and sliced, including tuna, salmon, and fluke. When eaten on its own, the raw fish is

In Japan, families celebrate Okuizome when babies are just more than three months old. At this age, they're still too young to eat solid foods, but the ceremony is meant to introduce them to traditional Japanese foods.

called sashimi. When served on top of individual rice portions or combined with ingredients such as seaweed, it's called sushi. A Japanese custom called Okuizome, or first meal, takes place 100 days after a baby is born. A full meal is served, including several fish dishes. The oldest family member of the same gender as the baby pretends to feed the infant a few bites. This ritual is meant to symbolize the importance of new life, family, and the culinary traditions that bring everyone together.

India has one of the largest populations in the world, and the country is full of richly flavored regional cuisines that are often dictated by religious beliefs. Some studies show that anywhere from 23 to 37 percent of Indians, many of whom are Hindu and believe cows are sacred, are vegetarian.[2] About 14 percent of Indians practice Islam, a religion that prohibits eating pork.[3] Meat may play a starring role in the flavorful stews known as korma or curry, but vegetarian versions are available as well. Most Indian food is served with rice and liberally seasoned with locally harvested herbs and spices, including black mustard seed, turmeric, ginger, garlic, and cardamom.

EUROPEAN CUISINE

From German bratwurst to Hungarian goulash to Polish pierogi, Europe is full of a variety of cuisines, each with its own cultural heritage. Popular in several countries surrounding the Mediterranean Sea, the Mediterranean diet dates to the ancient Greek and Roman civilizations. Because of the area's temperate climate and ample farmland, Mediterranean dishes such as stuffed roasted eggplant with couscous or charcoal-grilled chicken with quinoa are made from fresh ingredients with a long growing season, including tomatoes, pine nuts, olive oil, and garlic.

In Italy, Greece, and Spain, seafood dishes such as grilled octopus with lemon frequently appear on restaurant menus, each with their own regional twist. In northern Spain's Basque Country, for example, finger snacks called *pintxos*—which comes from the Spanish verb *pinchar*, meaning "to poke or stab"—are a staple of local food culture. On a typical Friday night in the bustling Spanish city of San Sebastián, groups of friends sample a variety of pintxos while visiting the city's taverns. One of the most popular pintxos consists of a spicy-sweet Guindilla pepper, a salty Cantabrian anchovy fillet, and a juicy Manzanilla olive on a skewer.

Unlike the lighter Mediterranean diet, heartier fare is more common in France. Rich stews such as beef bourguignon, wine-braised chicken coq au vin, or Provençal fish bouillabaisse are commonly served at French tables. Thanks to its abundant pastures, France is home to more than 1,000 varieties of cheese made from the milk of different animals, from cow's milk Vieux-Boulogne to sheep's milk Roquefort blue to goat's milk chèvre.[4] Fondue, a popular pastime in modern France that involves dunking bread in a pot of melted cheese, is a tradition dating to 800 BCE in the French and Swiss Alps. It began as a way for farmers to stretch their resources during the winter months.

MIDDLE EASTERN CUISINE

Throughout the world, Middle Eastern cuisine is renowned for its aromatic spices and enticing flavors. The region's food is influenced by its location at the intersection of Europe, Asia, and Africa and near the Mediterranean, Red, Arabian, and Caspian Seas. It is also affected by the vast trade routes

In San Sebastián, Spain, diners nibble on a meal of appetizers made with pickled vegetables, cured meats, crusty bread, and salty fish.

that have crisscrossed the area for centuries. In countries such as Jordan, Lebanon, Syria, Turkey, and Iran, cooks generously use spices including nutmeg, cumin, and saffron to create mouth-watering recipes. Musakhan is a popular Levantine dish made with roasted chicken, onions, sumac, and pine nuts on flatbread. Another favorite is tabbouleh, a Lebanese salad made with tomatoes, mint, onion, bulgur, chopped parsley, olive oil, and lemon juice.

In the arid Arabian Peninsula, where nomadic Bedouin tribes traditionally slow-cooked meats in underground sand

MANSAF: JORDAN'S NATIONAL DISH

Al-Mansaf is usually made with rice or bulgur wheat and lamb or goat meat. It is simmered in a rich sauce made from fermented yogurt. Its name comes from the word for "large tray" because it's served on a massive dish in the center of the table. During ancient times, warring tribal leaders marked the resolution of conflicts by sacrificing an animal and making Al-Mansaf together. It's still served in households as a way to calm tensions between family members.

pits and seasoned meals with spices picked up along trade routes, a culinary identity steeped in vibrant flavors and tender meats is present to this day. Saltah, Yemen's national dish, is prominent on Middle Eastern tables. Flavored with fenugreek, an herb that looks like a clover, this meat stew is most often eaten communally to celebrate the importance of family and generosity toward others.

AFRICAN CUISINE

All across Africa, home cooks and restaurant chefs alike take advantage of the continent's vast landscape, myriad climates, and diverse cultural heritage. The varied continent includes the highlands of eastern Africa, the bustling markets of western Africa, the ocean communities of northern Africa, and the savannah of southern Africa. Each region is known for its unique flavors and traditions. In the eastern African country of Ethiopia, for example, injera is a spongy, sour-tasting, fermented flatbread made from teff, a grain that's grown throughout the country. Injera is the foundation of many Ethiopian dishes and is often used in place of a utensil to scoop stewed vegetables or whatever else is on the plate.

Black-eyed peas, cassava and other root vegetables, and locally raised goat and chicken are staples in the western African diet. One-pot meals made in earthenware pots and cooked over an open fire are popular too. Jollof rice, a simmered rice-and-tomato stew flavored with thyme, Scotch bonnet peppers, onions, and garlic, is a versatile dish. It is commonly served at weddings, birthday celebrations, and holiday feasts all over Nigeria, Ghana, Togo, Senegal, and Gambia.

Many southern African dishes have roots in cuisine prepared by Indigenous peoples. One of the largest Indigenous groups is the Bantu, who grow

Injera, the spongy flatbread served at Ethiopian meals, is traditionally made on a griddle placed over an open fire.

pumpkins, beans, and other vegetables and raise goats, sheep, and cattle. Today, many South Africans cook a style of barbecue called braai on the weekend as a show of hospitality and to celebrate their community. One of the most popular days to braai is September 24, a holiday that's officially called Heritage Day but is also referred to as Braai Day.

> Africa produces nearly 220 million short tons (200 million metric tons) of cassava every year, more than half of the world's total production.[5]

CUISINE OF THE AMERICAS

Today, the phrase "American cuisine" may make people think of a hamburger and fries. But the reality is that food in the Americas is as different and unique as the continents' diverse populations. Long before the Europeans arrived, Indigenous peoples all over South America grew crops such as corn, sweet potatoes, chili peppers, and cocoa. They developed sophisticated irrigation methods so that crops could grow on the steep hillsides of the Andes mountain range. Many of these ingredients are still the foundations of modern South American recipes.

Feijoada, the national dish of Brazil, is a slow-cooked stew of black beans, roasted pork, and beef. In Colombia and Venezuela, arepas—corn cakes stuffed with beef, beans, or other fillings—can be part of every meal. In Peru, ceviche—a marinated seafood dish made with freshly caught fish, onions, and lemon juice—is typically served with sweet potatoes and large corn kernels called choclo.

Aside from featuring food from cultures all over the world, the United States does have a few native dishes. Fried chicken, collard greens, and shrimp and grits are staples at dinner tables in the Deep South. Plates piled high with crack-and-eat Maine lobster, local clams or mussels, roasted potatoes, and corn on the cob are mainstays at New England picnics during spring and summer. And people all over the country insist there's nothing more American than baked apple pie.

JOUMOU: A SYMBOL OF FREEDOM

In the Caribbean nation of Haiti, joumou isn't just a soup made with pumpkin or squash, beef, pasta, and other locally grown vegetables. It's a symbol of freedom. The dish was once a favorite of French plantation owners who had colonized the country and enslaved Haitian people. In 1804, Haitians revolted and earned their independence. Making this dish has become a tradition. Every New Year's Day, Haitians make joumou to celebrate their liberation from France.

CHAPTER THREE

THE GLOBALIZATION OF FOOD

When walking down a street in New York City, Chicago, or other major US cities, a visitor can choose from a wide range of restaurant options, from Cuban to Italian to Burmese. What's more, many of the spices, sauces, and produce used to create the dishes on these restaurants' menus are sourced from other countries. According to the US Food and Drug Administration, 55 percent of fresh fruits and 32 percent of fresh vegetables are imported from abroad.[1]

In return, many foods typically considered American have made their way around the world. The fast food restaurant McDonald's has locations in 118 countries.[2] The spread of food and epicurean traditions is made possible by globalization. Nations around the world have become connected through trade, technology, and the exchange of ideas.

Foods from around the world can be found in food stalls and street fairs throughout New York City.

Scott Lincicome and Sophia Bagley of the Cato Institute, a research organization, explain this phenomenon. They say, "Globalization expands our palates, fosters the sharing of diverse culinary traditions, and enables year-round access to fresh and healthy foods—championing free markets and transcending countries' often-stark geopolitical, cultural, and ideological divides."[3] This type of cultural culinary exchange occurs through three main avenues: colonization, immigration, and travel.

> In 2023, people in the United States bought 43.7 million servings of sushi at supermarkets and another 238.6 million servings at restaurants.[4]

COLONIZATION

An early example of gastronomic globalization in the Americas took place with the arrival of the Italian explorer Christopher Columbus in 1492. Up until that time, domesticated llamas, alpacas, guinea pigs, and turkeys roamed South America. In North America, the only domesticated animals were dogs. Crops grown in the Americas at that time included maize, cassava, and potatoes.

Sweet and hot peppers are native to the Americas. These fiery vegetables added spice to cuisines in European countries through trade with colonists.

In a centuries-long process later known as the Columbian Exchange, the European colonists shipped these and other crops, including tomatoes, sweet and hot peppers, cacao beans, and strawberries, back to the Old World, where people in Italy, Spain, France, and other countries had never seen them before.

In many instances, these New World crops influenced Old World dishes. In India, for example, people began to experiment with chili peppers from South America to make spicy curries. In Hungary, people used chili peppers to make paprika, and in Korea, chili peppers became a key ingredient

Ships were the only way to send fruits, vegetables, animals, grains, and other foods across the Atlantic. In the 1700s, it took about six weeks for a ship to make the voyage.

in kimchi. Tomatoes, which originated in South America more than 1,000 years before the Spanish arrived, became a key ingredient in Italian pasta dishes and pizza.

As more colonists made their way to the New World and brought their cooking skills with them, new imports began to arrive on American shores. Ships were loaded with wheat, rice, artichokes, eggplants, garlic, olives, apples, pears, and tea. In addition to fruits, grains, and vegetables, live animals arrived too, including pigs, ducks, cattle, sheep, goats, pheasants, and bees. "Imagine the American prairie with millions of buffalo but no wheat fields waving, Ohio and New York with no apple orchards . . . the Carolinas without rice paddies," says *Forbes* contributor John Mariani. "Such was the radical transformation of gastronomy on both sides of the world."[5]

Colonization inspired the intermingling of food-related ideas and customs. But colonization had its consequences as well. From the moment they arrived, European settlers warred with the Indigenous population for control of the region. They also inadvertently brought smallpox and measles, diseases the Indigenous people had never been exposed to. Between 1492 and 1600, approximately 90 percent of the Indigenous population died because of violence or illness.[6] This is about 55 million people.[7] Colonization affected the animal population too. Without any natural predators in the New World, many of the imported animals

A MIGHTY BEAN

The first cultivation of soybeans, which are native to Southeast Asia, dates back 5,000 years. In 1712, German botanist Engelbert Kämpfer learned about the crop and introduced it to Europe while working for the Dutch East India Company. In 1765, the bean traveled to the New World when British East India Company worker Samuel Bowen sent beans to a farmer friend in Georgia. Today, the United States, Brazil, and Argentina combined are responsible for more than 85 percent of global production of soybeans.[8]

reproduced by the hundreds of thousands, dominating and shaping the food chain of the future.

IMMIGRATION INFLUENCES

Like colonization, immigration has had a huge effect on food-related traditions around the world. Whenever big groups of people move from their country of origin to another country or continent, they bring their passed-down recipes, techniques, and ingredients with them. Some newcomers even open up restaurants. Over time, these food preferences and cooking styles evolve and spread. "Food is an important way for immigrants to find employment and share their cultural traditions and experiences, and it can promote liberty and mutual understanding through peaceful (and tasty) international exchange," Bagley says.[9]

Newcomers to the United States opened restaurants to make a living. New York City's Chinatown is home to the largest population of Chinese people in the Americas.

Throughout history, many examples are recorded of immigrants either directly or indirectly shaping the trajectory of the United States' food culture. In a tradition from the Indigenous Caribbean peoples, pigs were often roasted over open firepits as a pastime for families and neighbors. Today, that tradition still exists in US cities nationwide as barbecue.

Africans enslaved and taken to North America in the 1600s and 1700s brought yams and peanuts, which eventually became major cash crops for farmers in the South. After the American Civil War (1861–1865), Jewish immigrants from Eastern Europe brought such foods as latkes, pastrami, and knishes. With menu items such as hot pastrami or Reuben sandwiches, the deli is still one of the most popular restaurant styles in the United States today.

In Japan, sushi was originally sold as street food beginning around the 700s.[10] When many Japanese workers

THE DONUT KING

Many people consider Los Angeles, California, to be the donut capital of the United States. One of the people responsible for that honor is Ted Ngoy, who immigrated to California from Cambodia with his family in 1975 to escape genocide. He worked multiple service jobs until he had the idea to open a donut shop based on the Cambodian round cakes he ate growing up. As his success grew, he sponsored visas for other Cambodians fleeing the communist regime so they could open new locations. In 2022, roughly 80 percent of donut shops in Southern California were run by Cambodian immigrants.[11]

immigrated to the United States during the 1900s, they brought their traditions with them. In the 1960s, one of the first Japanese restaurants in the United States, Kawafuku, opened in Little Tokyo, a neighborhood in Los Angeles, California. It catered to Japanese businesspeople who had offices in the area. The restaurant spawned competition, which caused more Japanese restaurants to open in the surrounding area.

Before long, Hollywood celebrities had become fans of the food, and the popularity of sushi ballooned. By the 1980s, sushi restaurants were popping up across the country. Today, the food can even be found in grocery stores, sometimes in "Americanized" formats not traditionally made in Japan, such as California rolls.

After decades of immigration, the United States is a melting pot of ethnicities. It's a cornucopia of diverse flavors, tastes, and cuisines. "With all of [the immigrants]—from the . . . wheat-growing Swedes of the Plains and the Vietnamese . . . of Seattle, the cannoli-makers and pastrami-briners, the folders of phyllo and the smokers of trout, the pretzel twisters and the tortilla patters, every one of them has contributed to our vast and delectable potluck of so many wonderful things," says Mariani.[12]

FIGURES IN FOOD

Najmieh Batmanglij

When Najmieh Batmanglij was growing up in Iran during the 1940s, she wasn't allowed to join her mother in the kitchen to cook things such as fava beans and dill khoresh, a kind of beef stew. "Concentrate on your education," her mother would tell her. "There will be plenty of time for you to cook later in life."[13]

Her mother was right. After fleeing Iran during the fundamentalist revolution in 1979, Batmanglij and her husband moved to France, where she published her first cookbook of recipes given to her by her mother. In 1983, Batmanglij and her family immigrated to Washington, DC, where she wrote her first book in English, *Food of Life*.

Since then, she has written seven cookbooks, opened three restaurants including Joon, and won numerous prestigious awards. She has been called "the guru of Persian cuisine" by the *Washington Post* and one of "seven immigrant women who changed the way Americans eat" by the *New York Times*.[14]

Looking back on her career, Batmanglij is glad she could represent her culture. "Iranians are famous for the hospitality and kindness and they love to eat and celebrate," she says. "And so I want Iran associated with good things, and the best things are Iranian food."[15]

FOOD TOURISM

In today's globalized society, restaurants—many of which are owned or staffed by immigrants—showcase different gastronomies from all over the world. Still, one of the quickest ways to experience a culture's food and traditions in the kitchen is through travel. In addition to eating local food, tourists who want to learn about a country's food in a more meaningful way can participate in countless immersive cooking classes and culinary tours. "Food tourism is the act of traveling for a taste of place in order to get a sense of place," says Erik Wolf, executive director of the World Food Travel Association.[16]

One delicious and educational way to learn about a new culture is through hands-on cooking classes. All over the world, tour companies, culinary collectives, and individuals host workshops that teach tourists how to cook local traditional meals. Some classes even involve a trip to a nearby market for a taste of what shopping for the recipe looks, smells, and feels like. "If you've ever had the opportunity to travel afar and partake in a cooking class, a tasting, or a new dining experience, you already know that learning about the food of a culture is enriching," says Yetunde Oshodi-Fraudeau, founder of food tourism

Cooking classes offer a unique way to learn about different culinary traditions.

company Let's Eat the World. "Not only do you get to enjoy a richly delicious experience but you also walk away with a valuable way to deepen your understanding of that culture and its people."[17]

Another great way to learn about a culture through its food is by taking a food tour. In Hong Kong, travelers who book a tour with Little Adventures get a firsthand bite of all the best wonton shops in the city. No Footprints in India guides visitors through the winding, bustling pathways of Crawford Market, encouraging them to sip falooda—a cold drink made with ice cream, vermicelli noodles, jelly, rose syrup, nuts, and basil seeds—as they go. A three-hour walking tour run by Parrilla Tour in Buenos Aires, Argentina, introduces guests to choripán, a hot sausage sandwich; hand-cut, whole-knuckle beef pasties; and medium-rare Argentine beef with a side of puffy provoleta cheese.

Culinary festivals are a great way to sample foods from different cultures—and meet the people who make them. Oktoberfest, a world-famous festival held annually in Munich, Germany, is known for its beer, but it also draws people for the food. It usually runs from late September to the first weekend in October and celebrates everything Bavarian foodie culture has to offer, including hot pretzels and mustard, half-roasted chicken, roast ox, cheese spaetzle, and bratwurst. Pizzafest takes place every year in Naples, Italy—the birthplace of pizza. Attendees can sign up for pizza-making competitions and workshops and eat as many pieces as they can. First held in 1980, Taste of Chicago is the

FOODIE APPS

In addition to attending festivals and taking cooking classes, travelers interested in learning about food from other cultures can use social media apps. Feastly is designed to connect foodies with chefs who offer pop-up meals at the chef's home. VizEat invites users to connect with locals and attend dinner parties, walking tours, and cooking workshops. Roaming Hunger is a food-truck tracker that allows people to find food trucks in real time or book them for an event.

world's largest food-specific festival, with more than three million attendees every year.[18] Travelers can sample local dishes straight from the city's many ethnic neighborhoods at the nearly 100 food booths.

Whether it be sampling something from every booth in a food hall in Valparaíso, Chile, or going on a tour of a coffee farm in Bolivia, food is a gateway into understanding people from other countries and their cultures. "By traveling and experiencing different cuisines, you have the opportunity to broaden your horizons and make memories that will last a lifetime," Oshodi-Fraudeau tells people on her tours. "So, go ahead, embrace new culinary experiences, and let the food take you on a journey of discovery and cultural appreciation."[19]

CHAPTER FOUR

FOOD AND FAITH

As Sue McLaughlin, executive producer of the PBS series *The Meaning of Food*, puts it, "Our attitudes, practices, and rituals around food are a window into our most basic beliefs about our world and ourselves."[1] They can also reflect religious faith. In many of the major religions practiced in the United States and around the world, including Judaism, Islam, and Christianity, certain types of foods and specific meals have spiritual or even sacred significance. Other types of food are forbidden because of religious traditions.

JEWISH CULINARY TRADITIONS

For all Jewish people, many religious traditions surround food. Passover is an eight-day holiday that commemorates when the Israelites were freed from slavery in ancient Egypt. The Passover meal is called

Followers of many Eastern religions, including those of the Hindu-based religion Vaishnavism, honor special days by bringing food offerings to specific gods.

Jewish people observe Passover with a seder plate. It consists of a shank bone, a vegetable, an egg, bitter herbs, and haroseth, which is a sweet paste.

a seder, and during the meal participants sing songs and recite the story of the Exodus of the enslaved people from Egypt. They eat foods that symbolize the story, including matzo, which is unleavened bread, and bitter herbs called maror and chazeret.

In some Jewish sects, people follow a kosher tradition. According to the Pew Research Center, this includes 95 percent of Orthodox Jews.[2] The English word *kosher* comes from the Hebrew root *kashér*, which means "to be pure, proper, or suitable for consumption." To follow a kosher tradition means to eat according to the guidelines set down in the Torah, the Jewish book of sacred texts. People have been doing so for more than 3,000 years.

According to tradition, any meat consumed by a person who follows a kosher diet must come from the forequarters of ruminant animals, which are herbivores with a four-chambered stomach and split hooves. Examples include cows, sheep, goats, lambs, and deer. The animal must be slaughtered by a shohet, the Hebrew name for a person who is trained and certified to butcher animals according to Jewish laws. The blood must first be removed from the meat before preparation and consumption by soaking the meat in water for 30 minutes and salting it for an hour.

In a kosher diet, certain meats are strictly not allowed, including that of pigs, rabbits, squirrels, camels, kangaroos, and horses. No birds of prey such as scavenging poultry are permitted either. Meat or meat-derived products such as bone broth cannot be served in the same meal as dairy. Any utensils, plates, pots, or other kitchen equipment used to eat or prepare meat must be kept separate and used only for meat-related products. A separate set is used for dairy and fish.

THE PASSOVER PLATE

On every Passover table, a seder plate with five or six sections is placed in the center. Each section contains food that symbolizes an aspect of Passover. A roasted shank bone represents sacrifice; a roasted egg symbolizes the circle of life; bitter herbs stand for the bitterness of slavery; haroseth, which is a mixture of apples, nuts, and honey, represents the bricks and mortar used by the Jews to build structures in Egypt; and karpas, or parsley, symbolizes the success of Jews in Egypt before they became enslaved.

In addition to meat, dietary rules concern fish, seafood, vegetables, and dairy. Fish is considered kosher only if it comes from an animal that has fins and scales. Examples include tuna, salmon, halibut, or mackerel. Water-dwelling creatures that don't have fins, such as shrimp, crabs, oysters, lobsters, and other types of shellfish, are forbidden. Any dairy must come from a kosher animal. It can't contain any meat-related products such as gelatin, a gooey substance found in marshmallows and other desserts that is made from the hides and bones of pigs and cows, or rennet, an enzyme from the stomach lining of cows, sheep, or goats that's often found in cheese.

MUSLIM CULINARY TRADITIONS

Muslims also have guidelines regarding what they can eat. The Qur'an, the central religious text of Islam, categorizes certain foods as halal, which means lawful or allowable. Muslims believe animals should be well cared for and treated with respect and compassion. For this reason, Muslims can eat meat only if the animal is properly slaughtered while the name of Allah is pronounced. The blood must be fully drained from the animal.

Under Islamic law, other foods are considered haram, or forbidden. These include pork and pork by-products, any type of alcohol, and any food not prepared in a clean or hygienic way. Other haram ingredients include lard, which is made from pig fat, and gelatin. Cheese, yogurt, ice cream, or desserts that are made with rennet are also banned.

Similar to other religious groups, Muslims embrace or withhold food as a means of celebrating or honoring spiritual beliefs. Ramadan is the holiest time of year for Muslims, who fast, or refrain from any food or drink, during this time as a central part of their religious practice. It's a monthlong celebration that takes place during the ninth month of the Islamic calendar because this is when the Qur'an was first revealed to the

> **About 80 percent of US Muslims say that they fast during the holy month of Ramadan.[3]**

When the sun goes down, Muslim families gather to break their fast with the iftar meal.

Prophet Muhammad. The ninth month is when Muslims believe that the gates of heaven are open and the gates of hell are closed. This month of festivities is a time when people fast as a way to become closer to Allah, empathize with people who are less fortunate, and practice patience and gratitude.

During Ramadan, Muslims fast daily from sunrise to sunset. They eat a pre-fast meal called suhur before dawn. After sunset, they celebrate the breaking of the fast at iftar. Both meals are usually shared with family and friends in the community and contain foods such as bread, cheese, fresh fruit, vegetables, meats, and sweets. The types of

EID AL-FITR: A SWEET REASON TO CELEBRATE

At the end of every holy month of Ramadan, Muslims throw a three-day festival called Eid al-Fitr to celebrate the breaking of the fast. Everyone in the community gathers in the morning to recite Islamic prayers. People exchange gifts and make donations to those who are less fortunate. At night, there is a huge feast. Many energy-boosting sweets are served during the meal, including baklava and stuffed dates. Honey is a common ingredient because it was readily available during some of the earliest Eids in Saudi Arabia.

food served usually vary from region to region, but most suhur dishes are light and healthy to fuel the body with energy prior to fasting. "I try to keep my Ramadan very light and full of fiber, proteins, and complex carbs," says Muslim chef and food blogger Amanda Saab. "When Ramadan is during hot summer months, I also focus on hydrating foods."[4]

At the end of the day when the fasting is done, many Muslims snack on dates before the main meal for a quick, reviving energy boost.

CHRISTIAN CULINARY TRADITIONS

In the Christian tradition, the commemoration of Jesus's death and resurrection is considered to be the most sacred time of the year. The period of 40 days leading up to this period, stretching from Ash Wednesday to Easter Sunday, is called Lent. It represents Jesus's 40-day fast in the desert and his withstanding of temptations by the devil. During Lent, many Christians give up behaviors or certain foods as a way to reflect on Jesus's life, teachings, and suffering. Some Christians give up foods or beverages they enjoy, such as coffee, chocolate, or alcohol. Many Catholics don't eat meat on Ash Wednesday, Good Friday, or on any other Friday during Lent. Good Friday, the Friday before Easter Sunday, commemorates the day Jesus died on a wooden cross.

At the end of Lent, Christians celebrate Easter to commemorate the resurrection of Jesus Christ. Families and friends usually get together to prepare a large feast. Sometimes the meal includes eggs, which stand for Jesus's resurrection; roasted lamb, which symbolizes Jesus's sacrifice to God; and hot cross buns, sweet pastries with a cross on top to represent the cross on which Jesus was crucified.

Many Christian homes still decorate eggs on Easter as well, a tradition that dates to the 1200s. One explanation is that some Christians used to give up all meat and dairy during Lent. They painted the eggs red to symbolize Jesus's blood and the end of his suffering and then ate the eggs on Easter as a celebration of Jesus's life.

Another Christian practice happens several times a year during church services. In a ceremony known as the

Eucharist or Communion, Christians consume bread and wine that represent the body and blood of Jesus. The Eucharist derives from the Greek word *eucharistia*, which means "thanksgiving." Christians believe that the rite was initiated by Jesus the night before his crucifixion, when he served his disciples bread and wine.

OTHER RELIGIOUS CULINARY TRADITIONS

In addition to Jewish, Muslim, and Christian culinary traditions, other major world religions have many gastronomic customs. The Hindu faith embraces the idea of living in harmony with nature and having compassion for all creatures. This means that many Hindus don't include meat in their diet because they believe animals, particularly cows, are sacred.

Buddhism has no set dietary laws, and different schools of the spiritual practice follow different guidelines when it comes to food. But some Buddhists, such as those from the Mahayana sect in China, Taiwan, Vietnam, and Korea, are vegetarians. One of the five ethical teachings of Buddhism prohibits taking the life of any person or animal. Mahayana Buddhists follow this tenet strictly and refrain from eating meat to keep their bodies and thoughts pure and their spiritual path clean.

Other religions practice vegetarianism too. Rastafarians, who are part of a religious and political movement that began in Jamaica in the 1930s, eat only food that is ital, or free of chemicals and preservatives. Foods such as coffee, canned foods, and alcohol are forbidden. "Food's place at the heart of society has been a constant throughout societal development," says food blogger Joanna Sarah-Freedman. "While the specifics of our ritual eating may have changed in some cultures, food continues to define how we interact with one another."[5]

A BUDDHIST CULINARY TRADITION

Since the early days of Buddhism more than 2,500 years ago, people in countries such as Thailand, Cambodia, Myanmar, Sri Lanka, and Laos have cooked food to donate to monks. The practice is called giving alms. It's meant to foster a mutual relationship between the monks, who are sustained by the offerings so they can focus on their spiritual practice, and the donors, who believe giving alms promotes good fortune in their future life. In places such as Louangphrabang, Laos, the practice still exists today.

CHAPTER FIVE

ETHICAL DIETARY CHOICES

When it comes to dietary preferences, many people are open to eating anything or trying a food at least once. They eat meat, vegetables, dairy, and seafood. Some of these eaters don't consider how the animal was raised or the social justice issues surrounding food. They simply eat what they like.

But during the past 100 years, attitudes about diet have evolved in the United States. "For years, the number-one driving factor behind consumer food choices has been taste," says registered dietitian and nutritionist Marissa Thiry. "However, over time, value-driven consumers are weighing additional considerations, including social justice, animal welfare and environmental stewardship—all [of] which influence their food and beverage purchasing habits. As awareness and action

People choose to eat a vegetarian diet for different reasons, including concern about animal welfare or the environment.

continue to evolve, the idea of 'ethical eating' is becoming increasingly more mainstream."[1]

ANIMAL WELFARE CONCERNS

In 1906, writer Upton Sinclair published a novel called *The Jungle*. It was a fictional story based on the unsanitary, inhumane conditions of Chicago's stockyards at the time. Sinclair spent a year investigating conditions at the Union Stockyards after workers had gone on strike in 1904. He wanted to expose the problem and the oppression of Chicago's low-paid workers, so he spent several weeks inside some of Chicago's most notorious meatpacking plants and documented everything he saw.

He wrote about hundreds of animals being cramped into tiny spaces. The animals were covered in feces, and the walls were streaked with animal blood. There were toilets next to

Animals at Chicago's Union Stockyards were kept tightly packed together in small fenced areas where they could barely move.

meat-processing machines, and dead rats were swept into sausage meat.

When the novel was published, the public was outraged. This led to the first federal food safety laws in US history. The Meat Inspection Act of 1906 set sanitary standards for meat processing in slaughterhouses and transport between states. The Pure Food and Drug Act, also passed in 1906, required the sanitary production and labeling of anything consumed by the public. It led to the creation of the US Food and Drug Administration, the country's first consumer-protection agency.

As a result, consumer confidence in the safety of the food they purchased was mostly restored. The acts also established the concept of government oversight of the marketplace as a way to protect the public from harm. Today, the meatpacking industry is still one of the most regulated industries in the United States.

Regulation of food followed a similar path in the United Kingdom. In 1964, English writer Ruth Harrison published *Animal Machines*, a book that exposed the unsanitary and cruel practices in the livestock breeding and poultry farming industries. Public outcry in response to the book and pressure from the government prompted the UK Farm

Pasture-raised chickens have access to grassy pastures where the birds can roam at will, eating as many bugs as they like.

Animal Welfare Council to develop the Five Freedoms of animal welfare in 1965.

These freedoms stipulated that any animal has the right to be comfortable throughout its lifetime, even one destined for slaughter. This means they should be able to stand up, lie down, stretch, turn around, groom themselves, and be free of distress or discomfort, thirst or hunger, and pain or disease. These principles have been adapted and used around the world by farmers, ranchers, and others involved in food production to create animal-welfare protocols and regulate how animals are raised for food.

Today the ethical treatment of animals in food production is as important as ever, and some companies are labeling animal-related products accordingly. For example, most egg cartons have messaging that describes how the hens were raised. "Cage-free" means the birds were able to waddle around their henhouse before laying eggs. "Free-range" means the eggs come from cage-free hens that were allowed to go outside but might have been in small pens. "Pastured" or "pasture-raised" means the eggs come from hens that roam free on natural pastures.

In each of these cases, the living conditions aren't always clear-cut positive or negative. Pasture-raised hens can still be exposed to germs or violent interactions with other hens or wildlife. Still, the labels help consumers make educated decisions about which type of product is right for them.

GRASS-FED VS. GRAIN-FED MEAT

Today, about 80 percent of cattle are raised on grain-based products—usually corn and soy—in order to quickly fatten them.[2] Grain has more energy than a diet of grass or hay, so cattle grow larger. But grass-fed beef is lower in fat and higher in vitamins and antioxidants. It is also a more humane way of raising an animal for food because many cows raised on grass are pasture-raised, which means they are able to roam freely. Most cows with a grain-based diet are kept in small pens with little room to move.

SOCIAL JUSTICE ISSUES

In addition to weighing animal-welfare concerns, many people also consider social justice factors when making choices about food. According to the Food Ethics Council, a UK nonprofit group, many foods sold in the United States, such as coffee, chocolate, and certain fruits such as avocados and bananas, are grown overseas. In some origin countries, labor standards are not as rigorously enforced as they are in the United States. This can lead to unfair practices, such as child labor, forced labor, inhumane working conditions, low pay, and gender inequity.

In the chocolate industry, for example, 70 percent of the world's chocolate comes from cocoa beans grown in western African countries, mostly Ghana and the Ivory Coast. Since the

FAIRTRADE IN COCOA PRODUCTION

Cocoa was certified as a Fairtrade product in 1994. Farmers who participate in the program are paid a Fairtrade Minimum Price. This means that companies buying cocoa can't pay less than a certain amount, no matter how low the market price has dropped. Organically grown products receive a higher Fairtrade Minimum Price. On top of that price, farmers are paid a Fairtrade Premium. This money helps them improve their businesses by investing in new seedlings to replace old trees, building better facilities for crop collection and production, and optimizing storage and transportation methods.

1990s, journalists have exposed instances of widespread enslavement and child labor practices on cocoa farms in these countries. In Brazil, coffee industry workers earn 2 percent of the retail price for the coffee they grow to export. To make enough money to live, many families take their children out of school to work on the coffee plantations. In Honduras, nearly 40 percent of coffee plantation workers are children.[3] They work eight to ten hours a day and are often exposed to excessive heat, dangerous mechanical equipment, and toxic agrochemicals.

In light of these and other concerns, activists have called for policy reform to give more of the profit to the farmers, protect workers' rights, and ensure that ethical practices are in place at all stages of the supply chain, including growing, processing, and shipping. The standards created by Fairtrade International are one solution. The organization partners with 1.7 million farmers and workers in 75 countries to ensure they make a livable wage and are treated fairly.[4]

A product with the Fairtrade label means its producers and associated businesses have met these internationally agreed-upon, independently certified standards. "Buying Fairtrade means the product meets environmental, economic, and social standards that support and protect

Some people who work on coffee plantations have been subject to long workdays and difficult working conditions. Fairtrade International is one organization that is working to change these practices.

farmers and their communities from injustices, such as unfair wages, while also protecting the environment," says Thiry.[5]

ENVIRONMENTAL IMPACTS

According to the United Nations, about one-third of human-caused greenhouse gas emissions—a major contributor to climate change—is linked to food. The largest portion comes from agriculture and land use. Animal-based foods, such as red meat, dairy, and farmed shrimp, are widely considered to be the biggest offenders. For example,

GREENHOUSE GAS EMISSIONS PER 2.2 POUNDS (1 KG) OF FOOD[6]

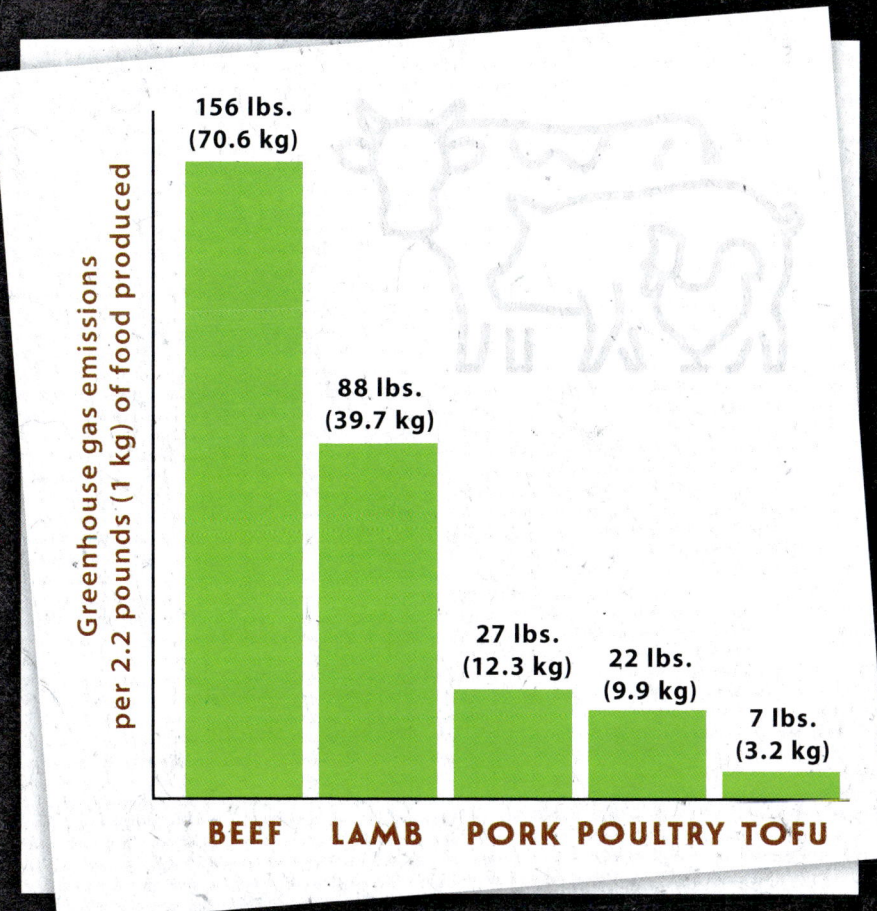

Beef has dramatically higher emissions than plants and other animals for three main reasons. Cows emit methane as they digest grass and plants, cattle manure releases nitrous oxide into the air, and grazing pastures are often created by cutting down trees, which releases carbon dioxide stored in forests.

cows, goats, and sheep discharge methane, a greenhouse gas, as they digest grass and plants. They also leave behind methane-rich manure throughout the pasture as they graze. For example, in one year a cow creates between 154 and 265 pounds (70 to 120 kg) of methane gas. More than 231 billion pounds (105 billion kg) of methane enters the atmosphere each year as a direct result of the 1.5 billion cattle raised for meat around the world.[7]

Industrialized farming methods, including the manufacturing, use, and disposal of pesticides, herbicides, insecticides, and artificial fertilizers, make up another major cause of climate change. While these agrochemicals protect crops from harmful diseases, pests, and invasive plant species, they can also damage the environment. They can cause deformities and negatively affect behavior in wildlife populations such as fish, birds, and insects. The chemicals can strip the soil of nutrients, making it unsuitable for further use. They can increase the production of nitrous oxide and ground-level ozone, greenhouse gases that can be toxic to humans, other animals, and plants.

Using these agrochemicals can also create a dependency cycle, meaning crops become reliant on pesticides to grow and ultimately require more pesticide use in the long run.

Asha Sharma is the organizing codirector for the Pesticide Action Network (PAN) North America. Sharma explains the connection between pesticide use and climate change: "We found essentially that climate change impacts are predicted to make pest pressures worse and make pesticides less effective, ultimately increasing pesticide use due to climate change, while at the same time pesticides release greenhouse gas emissions."[8]

Deforestation is a factor in climate change too. According to Greenpeace, a global nonprofit created to increase public awareness of environmental issues, 80 percent of global deforestation is the result of agricultural production, which is also the leading cause of habitat destruction.[9] For example, palm oil comes from the fruit of palm trees and is a key ingredient in

THE BENEFITS OF ORGANIC FARMING

Organic farming, which is growing crops without the use of synthetic fertilizers or pesticides, has been practiced in the United States since the late 1940s. Many farmers adopt these methods to encourage biodiversity, reduce erosion, improve soil fertility, and maintain soil structure across their land. By choosing to farm organically, they also reduce the risks of human, animal, and environmental exposure to toxic chemicals. According to the United States Department of Agriculture (USDA), the United States had about 17,445 organic farms in 2021.[10] That year there were 2,012,050 total farms in the United States.[11]

everything from shampoo to crackers. Clearing land for the production of palm oil removes the habitat of creatures like the orangutan, pygmy elephant, and Sumatran rhino in Indonesia and Malaysia. In coastal areas, shrimp farms have taken the place of mangrove forests, which absorb large amounts of carbon. When these mangroves are cut down to create shrimp farms, their stored carbon is released into the atmosphere as a greenhouse gas.

ETHICALLY RESPONSIBLE DIET CHOICES

When it comes to animal welfare, social justice, or environmental concerns, consumer food choices alone aren't going to solve the world's problems. But people can take steps to help mitigate the effects of issues such as climate change and animal cruelty. Making dietary changes is one of these steps. People may become vegetarians. Or they can become pescatarians, who do not eat land-based meat but do eat fish and shellfish. Or they can choose a vegan diet, refraining from eating,

According to a 2023 Gallup poll, 4 percent of Americans say they are vegetarian and 1 percent say they are vegan.[12]

wearing, or using any product that comes from an animal. People can also check food labels for signs that animals were raised using humane methods. Any of these choices can help reduce animal suffering and counteract negative environmental impacts.

Buying produce or goods directly from farmers helps support local agriculture by ensuring more money goes directly to farmers instead of to giant corporations. Purchasing food with Fairtrade certification helps ensure workers' rights are protected. Finally, paying attention to food labels, such as cage-free eggs, grass-fed beef, organic produce, and sustainable seafood not only helps keep people informed about where their food comes from but also contributes to an overall food production and consumption cycle that is healthier, more sustainable, and ethically sound.

Foods that abide by fair trade practices are clearly marked with the Fairtrade logo.

CHAPTER SIX

FARM TO TABLE

When thinking about buying food, many people picture going to a small grocery store or large supermarket. But since the mid-1970s, food shopping patterns have changed. Now people can choose from a number of ways to get their food, including direct-to-consumer farmers markets, community-supported agriculture (CSA) programs, and even volunteering at local farms.

A TRIP TO THE FARMERS MARKET

Farmers markets, places where farmers from different locations can sell directly to consumers, aren't exactly new, even in the United States. As early as 1730, urban planners in Lancaster, Pennsylvania, included a lot in the center of town that would serve as the Lancaster Central Market. Over time, it grew to include 400 vendors selling

Farmers markets provide a public space where local growers can sell their products.

The Union Square Greenmarket in New York City began with a handful of farmers in 1976. It's become a place for growers to connect with restaurant owners and families.

everything from fresh produce to meat to shoes. The market was so popular that it led to dozens of smaller markets around the city, with merchants and farmers selling their goods until after World War I (1914–1918). The Market House, the building in which the Lancaster Central Market is located, was built around 1889.

Farmers markets are still going strong. In 2024, more than 8,600 farmers markets were operating nationwide.[1]

The markets offer everything from fresh, locally grown fruits and vegetables to locally sourced eggs, meat, and fish. Vendors sell homemade baked goods such as muffins, bread, and pies as well. Some larger or specialty markets feature goods not normally found in a regular supermarket, including handmade soaps and even handcrafted wares such as crocheted bags, stained-glass art pieces, and hand-carved cheese boards.

But the farmers market isn't just a place to buy groceries or arts and crafts. It has evolved into a social meeting place for people in the surrounding communities. At some markets, musicians play for people as they shop. Others have pop-up restaurants or made-to-order food from local chefs. People can buy produce, eat lunch, and listen to music for an entire afternoon.

In addition to fostering togetherness and community, farmers markets have proven to be a good way for farmers to connect with prospective clients. Zaid Kurdieh owns Norwich Meadows Farm in Norwich, New York. He also has a booth at the Union Square Greenmarket in New York City, one of the oldest US farmers markets. Because of his social interactions with chefs and restaurant owners at the market, 50 percent of his business

THE BIGGEST US FARMERS MARKET

The Dane County Farmers' Market in Madison, Wisconsin, is the largest US producers-only farmers market. Founded in 1972, it had about 275 participating members in 2024. Every Wednesday and Saturday from April through November, anywhere from 150 to 170 vendors sell their wares.[2] These include everything from award-winning cheese and cheese curds to pickles and jams to chocolate chip cookies to dog treats and pork. There's even a farmers market cookbook of recipes that feature local ingredients and stories from the farmers, chefs, and shoppers in the Dane County community.

goes to people who work in the restaurant industry. "We have a lot of relations with a lot of different people, and that is because of the farmers market," he said. "Without this showcase, if you will, our showroom here, we wouldn't be able to do some of the things that we do."[3]

COMMUNITY-SUPPORTED AGRICULTURE

Community-supported agriculture has been popular in the United States since the 1980s. It works by allowing people in a farm's surrounding community to become members by purchasing shares in the farm's future harvests. People pay a price for their share at the beginning of the growing season. This amount is usually anywhere from $400 to $700, depending on the location of the farm and the products it offers.[4] This up-front payment helps farmers buy seeds to plant the season's harvest and provides money for necessary expenses to run the farm, such as equipment repair.

In exchange for their membership fee, farm shareholders receive a container of freshly picked produce every week or month. Some shareholders pick up their produce at the farm or a local pickup spot. Others may have it delivered to their door. If the farm is organically certified, the selection of goods will also be organic.

Some CSAs offer other goods. In addition to traditional items, CSAs at Sweet Eats Farm in Maidstone, Vermont, can include honey, maple syrup, nuts, and dairy products including cheese and milk. Moon River Ranch in Clinton, Montana, offers soap and body care products, plant seedlings, and cut flowers in its weekly boxes.

The benefits of belonging to a CSA are numerous. Members can feel confident that they're eating healthy, sustainably grown food and using environmentally friendly products because they know where the food and products come from. Farmers can gain connections in the community and get help with their business expenses and cash flow. Many farms that run CSAs offer educational programs

CSA members go to a central location to pick up their farm share once a week. Shares might include flowers, vegetables, fruits, and handmade items.

and social activities too. Seed to Table in Sisters, Oregon, has farm teacher training, adult gardening workshops, a youth summer camp, and community planting, harvesting, and cooking days.

WHAT IS WWOOFING?

People who want to get hands-on experience and learn what it's like to work on an organic farm can get involved with an intensive volunteer program called WWOOF, which stands for Worldwide Opportunities on Organic Farms. Founded in 1971, the WWOOFing movement was created to allow people greater access to organic farmers and build a global community of people who care about eco-friendly farming practices. Today, participating farms are in more than 132 countries across the globe.[5]

TEIKEI: THE FIRST CSA

Community-supported agriculture began in the 1960s in rural Japan. Japanese philosopher Teruo Ichiraku traveled from village to village to educate people about the dangers of using pesticides and other chemicals in farming. A group of Japanese women heard his lessons and joined to form the first *teikei*, a partnership dedicated to learning about farming and eating food grown on local farms. The first CSA in the United States formed in Massachusetts in 1984. By 2024, the country had more than 4,000 CSAs.[6]

People who participate in the WWOOFing program don't get paid for their work. But they do get free meals and a place to stay. For up to 25 hours per week, volunteers are encouraged to take part in the farm's daily activities, such as milking cows, planting and harvesting vegetables, and caring for farm animals so they can learn what it takes to run a successful farming business. Some even work the booths at farmers markets. WWOOF participants pay a minimal annual membership fee depending on which country they choose—in the United States, it's $40—and no prior farming experience is required.[7]

> **Since the WWOOF program started in 1971, the number of participating farms has grown to 12,000 in more than 130 countries.[9]**

Rose, a WWOOFer, spent three months volunteering on a farm-to-table, 256-acre (104 ha) camp and farm in the mountains of Julian, California. While there, she weeded and mulched beds, planted garden seeds, pruned trees, processed herbs, learned about composting, and cared for farm animals. "I have engaged with beautiful knowledge about caring for land and animals that I will carry with me always," Rose says of her experience.[8]

WWOOFers may help harvest vegetables, plant seeds, or care for animals.

WHITE OAK PASTURES: A ONE-STOP SHOP

Whether it's hosting a fully stocked farm stand, selling his grass-fed beef directly to consumers online, or managing the interns who work at White Oak Pastures (WOP), Will Harris has done it all. Harris is a fourth-generation rancher in Bluffton, Georgia, on the same 5,000 acres (2,023 ha) his great-grandfather settled in 1866. He's spent the past 30 years working to transition his farm from one that relied on pesticides and synthetic chemicals into the zero-waste, regenerative-farming model it is today.[10] WOP raises ten species of livestock on open pastures, allowing the animals

A RETURN TO REGENERATIVE FARMING

Will Harris has long been a spokesperson for the benefits of regenerative farming. In 2023, he published a memoir about his life called *A Bold Return to Giving a Damn: One Farm, Six Generations, and the Future of Food*. It got rave reviews, including this one from a reporter at the *Washington Post*: "It's Harris's dogged insistence on explaining the hidden costs of the 'abhorrently cheap food' that industrial farming makes possible—the negative health effects of hormones on animals and humans, runoff pollution in streams, the collapse of rural farming towns—that makes the book so necessary."[12]

to express their natural behaviors; grows organic vegetables; and produces honey. It is also one of the only US farms to operate two on-farm, USDA-inspected slaughterhouses for red meat and poultry in order to ensure a humane end of life for their animals.

With WOP, Harris has created a tightly run ship that has earned him a reputation as "one of the most successful purveyors of grass-fed, humanely raised beef in the country," according to the *New York Times*.[11] But he has also done a great deal to give back to the community. The farm employs more than 155 people who live in Bluffton. A general store sells products made from the farm, and a farm-to-table restaurant is right behind it. Rustic cabins are available for visitors who want to book a farm tour, go for a trail ride, or take one of the many educational workshops the farm has to offer, including classes on soil-health management, leather shoemaking, and beekeeping.

Beth Hoffman, an Iowa-based farmer who visited the farm in 2022, was struck by the sense of community at WOP. Hoffman says, "As I stood in the street . . . chatting with 20- and 30-somethings from around the country who have flocked to this tiny town in the middle of nowhere, I couldn't help hope our own farm will be able to build a fraction of the community what WOP has. They have created true livelihoods in a place where none existed."[13]

CHAPTER SEVEN

THE DINING EXPERIENCE

Going out for dinner has traditionally meant walking or taking transportation to a brick-and-mortar restaurant with family or friends, ordering a dish off the menu, and then leaving the table at the end of the meal, hopefully satisfied and stuffed. But these days, many ways to enjoy a scrumptious meal or unique dining experience go beyond the traditional concept. They range from an incredibly fancy tasting menu experience or a meal prepared by a world-renowned chef to the sometimes dirt-cheap but delicious dinner from a food truck. Modern diners have more choices than ever before.

THE TASTING MENU

As one of the fanciest dining experiences, tasting menus invite guests to explore a full range of

Artfully assembled salads, main dishes, and desserts add to the multi-course tasting menu experience.

Traditional sushi chefs train for ten years, spending two to three years alone on perfecting the rice.

impeccably prepared foods. These multi-course meals can include anywhere from three to dozens of dishes showcasing a variety of styles and flavors to highlight a chef's skill and creativity. Most tasting menus evolve over time to feature seasonal ingredients and the chef's latest inspirations. The dining experience can last anywhere from an hour to an entire evening.

When Empire State South in Atlanta, Georgia, was open, it had a tasting menu consisting of six dishes. "Sometimes it's comprised of dishes fully on the menu, and sometimes it's got new additions and different things [the chef] is playing around with. And it's always a showcase of technique, and the idea of the food that [we're] really into at that time," said owner Hugh Acheson. "I think it's a bit of a magical thing, though, to have a dinner that's that many courses, interesting, and then surprises in between, and sort of a change up for our staff to be professional in a different way."[1]

At Sushi Sho in Honolulu, Hawaii, Japanese sushi master Keiji Nakazawa serves up to 40 different types of raw fish and different styles of rice in 32 separate courses selected by the chef. Ten diners eat at the sushi bar in front of the sushi chefs. The experience takes many hours to complete and costs $300 per person.[2] Reservations must be made up to a year in advance.

But not all tasting-menu restaurants are extravagant or extremely expensive. In recent years, some restaurateurs have chosen to make the tasting-menu

A SWEET TASTING MENU

Tasting menus are normally reserved for delicacies such as small plates of sushi or impeccably prepared bites of steak. But there are also options for diners with a sweet tooth. Bellaria Dessert Studio, a small, cozy restaurant in San Francisco, California, serves up a three-course dessert tasting menu at $65 a seat.[3] In the past the menu has featured delectable offerings such as tiramisu filled with mascarpone cheese, soufflé bread pudding, and chocolate mousse. The meal starts with savory treats such as mushroom popovers and ends with a bite-size piece of homemade chocolate.

experience more affordable for diners, especially since the COVID-19 pandemic began. For example, Zacchaeus Golden runs Southern Soigné in Jackson, Mississippi. It's in a homelike environment, and the only other employee is his mother. The cottage is decorated with art by local artists. The cost of the seven-course meal is $95 per person with a three-course option for $65. "What the new generation of tasting-menu restaurants lack in luxury trappings, they make up for with nervy imagination conveyed by deeply personal food, bohemian charisma, and business models that challenge assumptions about what restaurants should provide customers and employees," says *New York Times* reporter Brett Anderson.[4]

FOOD TRUCK MANIA

Since 2008, another gastronomic trend that has caught on in the United States and around the world is the food truck, a truck or trailer that's outfitted with all the equipment needed to store, transport, cook, serve, and sell food to the public. Cities including Los Angeles, Chicago, and New Orleans, Louisiana, have collections of food trucks called pods. There, individual business owners prepare dishes with origins from all corners of the globe—all in the same parking

FIGURES IN FOOD

Charlie Mitchell

In 2019 Charlie Mitchell, a self-trained chef from Detroit, Michigan, was set to take a job in Norway. He was in his late twenties and working two jobs to save up for the trip. But then the COVID-19 pandemic began, and his plans fell apart. After a bit of scrambling, he took a job as the executive chef of Clover Hill, a 20-seat restaurant in Brooklyn, New York. "I felt that I'd be doing myself a disservice not to at least try," Mitchell said about the choice.[5]

Less than a year after Clover Hill opened, the decision had already paid off. Mitchell became the first Black chef in New York City to be awarded a Michelin star, the highest honor in the culinary world. He's only the second Black chef in the United States to receive it. In 2023, Mitchell was named a James Beard Emerging Chef finalist, another badge of honor.

In an interview about the accolades, Mitchell said he owed his love for cooking and his success to his grandmother, who was born and raised in Macon, Georgia. The time he spent cooking with her influenced the types of dishes he creates today, such as king salmon with tapioca and ginger purée, dry-aged Rohan duck, or shima aji potato and caviar. "I saw how happy food made people and decided I could do it for a living," he said.[6]

Patrons line up to sample foods from around the world from food trucks parked in San Francisco, California.

lot or block of a city. With seemingly endless options, patrons can enjoy a meal from a different place every time, such as sushi burritos from Japan, tamales from Mexico, barbecue ribs from Texas, or falafel from the Middle East.

A food cart pod has many benefits—for diners and chefs alike. Start-up costs for food trucks range between $75,000 and $250,000, making a truck much cheaper than financing a brick-and-mortar restaurant.[7] Operating costs are also lower. Plus, compared with a regular restaurant, a food truck has fewer staff to pay. It's an all-around economic win.

Food trucks are also an easy way to engage with the public. As writer Katherine Boyarsky explains, "They offer food truck owners the opportunity to share original food concepts with a wider audience. Mobile food service brings a high degree of flexibility to how you can operate and engage with your community."[8]

One city known for its legendary food truck pod scene is Portland, Oregon. More than 600 carts are spread throughout the city. In Portland, carts aren't required to move or be stowed away for the night as they are in other places such as New York City.

Cart operators can serve anything from prepackaged food and beverages to unpackaged food that is prepared and cooked elsewhere to a full menu that's diced, simmered, or fried right in the cart's mini kitchen. "To me, the best part of having so many food carts is the great diversity in cuisine," says Sherri, a tour guide who writes for the food blog *Portland by Mouth*. "It would be very

THE CHUCK WAGON: FIRST FOOD CARTS

Food trucks may seem like a modern invention in the United States, but they actually date to the American Civil War. Horse-drawn carriages called chuck wagons were like mobile kitchens that fed cowboys who were leading livestock on trails to markets in other states. Texas rancher Charles Goodnight was believed to be the first to come up with a prototype. At the back of the wagon was a "chuck box," a box with a lid that provided a flat cooking surface. The box contained drawers to hold cooking supplies, and a Dutch oven was housed underneath.

easy to feel like you've traveled around the world eating, while staying in a one block radius. And a lot less hassle than a long plane ride."[9]

WILD AND WACKY FOODIE EXPERIENCES

If ordering food from a truck isn't novel enough, people have many other options available to enjoy food with friends or family in a truly original and wacky way—if they're willing to travel. At Hurawahli Island Resort in the Maldives, guests can enjoy their meal while sitting in a dining room that's 19 feet (5.8 m) under the sea. Called 5.8, the restaurant is the world's largest all-glass underwater eatery, seating 16 people at a time.[10] The meal consists of a seven-course seafood menu and lasts for more than three hours.

> **In 2023 there were 47,033 food trucks operating in the United States. It was a $2.2 billion industry.[11]**

Located within the Arctic Circle in Rovaniemi, Finland, the aptly named Ice Restaurant is made completely of ice. Specialties on the menu include velvety forest mushroom soup, braised Arctic Ocean salmon, and roast elk. Guests are encouraged to wear coats, hats, and boots to their three-course meal. After dining, they can stay overnight in the adjacent Arctic SnowHotel or in glass igloos, where the rooms and bed frames are made out of ice too. Warm sleeping bags are provided.

If diners prefer something strange but slightly more low-key, Seattle is home to a restaurant where guests can dine in the dark. Patrons are blindfolded throughout the entirety of the three-course meal so they can't see what they're eating or how to eat it. Tickets to this event are $90, and diners can choose between three types of meals: vegan, seafood, or meat. "Fantastic and well-thought experience," says one reviewer about her dining experience. "Really had to rely on other senses to get your way through the table. . . . Had a great time and would recommend to all!"[12]

DINNER IN THE SKY

One of the most bizarre dining experiences in the world involves eating an hourlong meal with strangers while seated at a large covered table hoisted by a crane and suspended 180 feet (55 m) above the city streets below it.[13] The idea, called Dinner in the Sky, originated in Belgium in 2007. Since then it has expanded to cities as far-flung as Dubai in the United Arab Emirates and São Paulo in Brazil. The concept was so successful that the company now does weddings in the sky too. The one requirement is that guests must not be afraid of heights.

CHAPTER EIGHT

THE FUTURE OF FOOD CULTURE

According to the United Nations Environment Programme (UNEP), nearly ten billion people will likely be living on the planet by 2050.[1] Yet in 2022, up to 40 percent of all cropland worldwide was facing soil erosion, livestock overgrazing, and reduced fertility.[2] "When we think about threats to the environment, we tend to picture cars and smokestacks, not dinner. But the truth is, our need for food poses one of the biggest dangers to the planet," says environmental scientist Jonathan Foley. "The environmental challenges posed by agriculture are huge, and they'll only become more pressing as we try to meet the growing need for food worldwide."[3]

As Earth's climate evolves and more extreme weather patterns affect how food is grown, many scientists, farmers, politicians, and neighborhood

Rooftop gardens are one way to grow more food in urban areas.

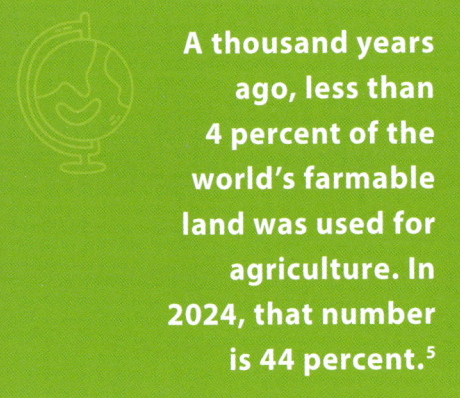

A thousand years ago, less than 4 percent of the world's farmable land was used for agriculture. In 2024, that number is 44 percent.[5]

groups agree that changes are needed to ensure these billions of people can be fed. Movements are already underway to find innovative, sustainable ways to produce food while also conserving energy and resources. While not all sides agree on the specific methods, most people support the idea that doing something is better than ignoring the problem. "We would be wise to explore all of the good ideas, whether from organic and local farms or high-tech and conventional farms, and blend the best of both," Foley says.[4]

INNOVATIVE FARMING INITIATIVES

Throughout history, people have traditionally cut down forests or plowed up grasslands to clear the land and make it suitable for growing crops and raising animals. Some estimates show that the total amount of land cleared for farming is about the size of South America. The amount of land cleared to make room for grazing livestock is about the size of Africa.

About half of the world's population lives in cities. By 2050, that amount is expected to jump to 70 percent, according to the United Nations.[6] Many of these urban dwellers currently face food shortages or will have limited access to affordable, healthy food in the future.

In light of these issues, hundreds of organizations and communities around the world are working together to find solutions for food shortages and a host of other related problems. Founded in 2014 by Angel Adelaja, the Nigerian company Fresh Direct is closing the gap between agriculture and the urban markets in which crops are sold by bringing farming to cities.

The group installs vertical stacking planters in homes and businesses and uses hydroponics, a soil-less technique in which crops are grown in nutrient solutions, so the

A GREEN ROOF OPEN TO THE PUBLIC

Colorado State University in Fort Collins, Colorado, is home to one of the largest research-dedicated green roofs in the United States. Each year, it attracts thousands of visitors who want to learn about farming. Students and members of the public can explore and get their hands dirty in each of its four sections. They include a 576-square-foot (54 sq m) food production area planted with tomatoes, peppers, cilantro, cucumbers, and other vegetables, and another area dedicated to medicinal herbs.[7] In addition to hosting educational programs, the rooftop provides food for many underserved members of the surrounding community.

farming process is more accessible to everyone. Through these methods, Fresh Direct has made it possible to get as much as ten times more yield using the equivalent of 7 percent of the land that would normally be used in a traditional farming method.[8]

Another company, Gotham Greens, builds climate-controlled greenhouses in cities across the United States. The greenhouses are powered by wind and solar energy and grow herbs and vegetables year-round, using fewer resources than traditional farming. Gotham Greens partners with local organizations, community gardens, and schools to educate the public about sustainable farming issues and to recruit volunteers. It was also the first company in the United States to build a commercial greenhouse on a roof. It's located on top of the Brooklyn Whole Foods store in New York City.

BEEF MADE IN TEST TUBES

According to the American Museum of Natural History, the global livestock industry uses 75 percent of all farmable land for grazing and growing food for animals. It produces at least 18 percent of total greenhouse gas emissions.[9] Some food scientists suggest that developing meat in labs using animal cells would reduce the impact of raising so many live animals to satisfy global demand. "I think the answer is, you make real meat in exactly the same taste and texture that people are used to, but you make it in a way that doesn't require billions of animals," says Josh Tetrick, CEO of Eat Just, a company pursuing lab-grown meat.[10]

Shifting from traditional beef production methods to growing meat in labs could reduce the amount of methane released into the atmosphere.

There's already an array of plant-based meat products, such as Impossible Burgers and Beyond Chicken Tenders, available on supermarket shelves. Business partnerships are underway to bring lab-grown meat to a few select restaurants too—and the cost of producing it is going down. In 2013, the first burger made of lab-grown meat cost $325,000 to create. By 2022, that price had dropped to less than $50, and it's still dropping.[11] Some experts estimate that by 2040, lab-grown meat, chicken, and pork may account for 35 percent of the global meat market.[12]

SUSTAINABLE FISH FARMING

Oceans are an essential part of the world's ecosystems. But a number of factors, including climate change, pollution, habitat degradation, and overfishing, are beginning to threaten their survival. In the fishing and seafood industry, organizations are working to counteract the negative effects of overfishing wild fish and seafood by developing new types of aquatic farms.

Unlike traditional cage or pen fish farms, which use wild fish for feed and can cause pollution and spread disease, new aquaculture methods rely on a closed system that's cleaner and less resource intensive. "Through aquaculture growth, consumers from low- to high-income nations have benefited from year-round availability and access to aquatic foods, which are rich in protein and micronutrients," says Rosamond Naylor, a researcher at the Center on Food Security and the Environment at Stanford University.[13]

Sustainable fish farms in the ocean allow a natural flow of water through the pens while removing algae and waste before it mixes with the ocean water.

In Singapore, a start-up called Vertical Oceans grows

shrimp, fish, and algae in water-filled urban towers without the use of pesticides, disinfectants, or antibiotics. Israeli start-up Sea2Cell incubates fish cells in massive tanks and uses the cells to grow fish meat. In the United States, nationwide oyster shell recycling programs are encouraging restaurants and their patrons to help restore wild oyster reefs and support the next generation of native oysters. After the oyster shells are collected from restaurants and put back into the ocean, they provide a nesting place for oyster larvae to latch on to and begin growing their own shells.

COMMUNITIES RALLY AROUND OCEAN HEALTH

In 2004, David Rockefeller Jr. cofounded Sailors for the Sea, a group in Rhode Island dedicated to helping boaters and water-sport enthusiasts in the community reduce their environmental impact on the ocean. Twenty years later, the group had 71,000 members and outposts in Japan, Portugal, and Chile. One of its most popular programs is Kids Environmental Lesson Plans (KELP), which teaches kids about ocean health. The program has reached 4,700 organizations, schools, and families, as well as 380,000 children across all 50 US states and in 76 countries.[14]

NEW FOOD CHOICES

In addition to the varied new ways to source food, the types of foods humans are eating are evolving. According to the American Museum of Natural History, approximately 2,500 plant species have already been domesticated for food. But despite that figure, nearly half of humans' food calories still come from three sources: rice, maize or corn, and wheat. "What about the thousands of overlooked plant species—and an untapped diversity of animals?" the museum's *Future of Food* exhibit asks. "These resources could provide solutions to problems like the need for resilience in our food production systems and the need to meet growing demands without depleting natural resources."[15]

Different types of grains, such as pest- and disease-resistant emmer wheat, could add to the diversity of cultivated crops. Emmer wheat, which was first cultivated 10,000 years ago, is being grown in places such as India and Nepal because it can grow in less fertile soil. This variety can also withstand climate disasters better than standard wheat and other modern counterparts.

Another option for sustainable plant sources exists in seas and oceans. Seaweed and algae, already consumed regularly in countries such as Japan, are popping up in restaurants and households across the globe thanks in part to the rise in the popularity of sushi. These nutritious aquatic plants are considered more sustainable than other crops because they don't require farmland or fresh water to grow and can easily thrive without the use of potentially harmful chemical fertilizers or pesticides.

Insects have also become a popular snack choice in some cultures. A whopping 2,000 species of insects are already being munched on worldwide, including caterpillars in South Africa, bee larvae in Vietnam, crickets in Cambodia, and cockroaches in Madagascar.[16] And these types of bugs not only are high in protein but also require fewer resources to grow and survive than livestock.

Seaweed farming, which has become a reliable source of nutrition in Asian countries, could provide sustainable food throughout the world.

FOODIE INVENTIONS

In some respects, humans have come a long way since hunting with a bow and arrow or taking the first garden hoe to the soil. In the 2020s, many companies are working to understand what people will want to eat in the future and how to meet those desires in ways that are environmentally

GROSS BUT GOOD?

In some parts of the world, entomophagy—the act of eating bugs—is considered gross. But in fact, insects are among the healthier creatures humans can eat because they are high in protein and other nutrients such as omega-3 fatty acids. People in Mexico regularly snack on crunchy grasshoppers and call them *chapulines*.

and socially responsible. "They're forming partnerships with chefs, doing a better job understanding how and where people eat, what they want food to taste like, how to help people transition into more healthful, sustainable diets that don't feel like a huge compromise," says food industry consultant Sarah Sha. "They're trying to make a healthy diet more of an exciting celebration, rather than feeling deprived."[17]

Some promising scientific and agricultural developments may seem outlandish but may come to fruition. Edible water bottles made out of water and sodium alginate, a thickening agent found in brown algae, can help reduce the nearly 441 million short tons (400 million metric tons) of plastic produced each year.[18] Color-changing "smart" food packaging made from biodegradable corn protein, starch, and other naturally derived materials can determine whether a food has spoiled by detecting enzymes from bacteria such as *E. coli* and listeria on the item's surface.

There's even a heat-resistant coffee bean in the works that will flourish in higher temperatures—a must for coffee cultivation on a warming planet. "It's not going to be in coffee shops in the next couple of years," Aaron Davis, head of coffee research at the Royal Botanic Gardens, Kew, told the British Broadcasting Corporation (BBC) in 2022. "But I think within five to seven years we'll see it entering the market as a niche coffee, as a high value coffee, and then after that I think it will be more common."[19]

EMBRACING WHAT'S NEXT

Gathering with family or friends to cook and enjoy a meal has long been an integral part of human life. These days, with the rapid increase in population, ever-present threat of climate change, and dwindling ecological resources, the food choices people make have become an important aspect of culture too. Whether it's dining at farm-to-table restaurants, opting to become a vegetarian, or supporting a nonprofit organization engaged in more sustainable fishing or farming practices, the decisions people make about food can have a global impact.

ESSENTIAL FACTS

GLOBAL FOOD

- Beyond keeping humans alive, food is a symbol of humanity's deep connection to history, culture, and national pride.

- The spread of food and epicurean traditions occurs through three main paths: colonization, immigration, and travel.

- Some people, including Orthodox Jews, Muslims, and Hindus, have dietary restrictions related to their faith.

- Diners can get unique cultural experiences by dining at esteemed restaurants, food carts, restaurants with tasting menus, and more.

FOOD PRACTICES

- There are many people who choose a vegetarian, vegan, or pescatarian diet because of concerns about social justice, animal welfare, or environmental impact.

- The Meat Inspection Act of 1906 set sanitary standards for meat processing in slaughterhouses and transport between states.

- The Pure Food and Drug Act of 1906 required the sanitary production and labeling of anything consumed by the public and led to the creation of the US Food and Drug Administration, the country's first consumer-protection agency.

- Buying Fairtrade products and shopping at farmers markets are ways to support fair treatment of farmers and equal pay.

GOOD FOR THE PLANET

- According to the United Nations, about one-third of human-caused greenhouse gas emissions—a major contributor to climate change—is linked to food.

- Consumers have many options for getting food outside of standard supermarkets, including direct-to-consumer farmers markets, community-supported agriculture programs, and even volunteer time at a local farm.

- As much as 40 percent of all cropland worldwide is facing soil erosion, overgrazing because of livestock, and reduced fertility.

- Some food innovations in development include lab-made beef, vertical fish farming, edible water bottles, urban greenhouses, and smart food packaging.

QUOTE

"If you've ever had the opportunity to travel afar and partake in a cooking class, a tasting, or a new dining experience, you already know that learning about the food of a culture is enriching. Not only do you get to enjoy a richly delicious experience but you also walk away with a valuable way to deepen your understanding of that culture and its people."

—*Yetunde Oshodi-Fraudeau, founder of food-tourism company Let's Eat the World*

GLOSSARY

agrochemical
A chemical such as an insecticide, herbicide, or synthetic fertilizer that is used in agriculture to protect crops from pests, invasive species, and other threats.

aquaculture
The process of raising fish and other aquatic animals for food.

biodiversity
The number of different plants and animals in an ecosystem.

composting
Recycling organic matter, such as leaves and food scraps, into a fertilizer that can enrich soil and plants.

cornucopia
A large supply of something, such as vegetables or flowers.

cuisine
The cooking methods and food traditions of a particular group of people.

dietitian
An expert in nutrition.

epicurean
Having good taste when it comes to eating and drinking; an adjective used to describe food-related subjects or topics.

gastronomic
Related to the practice of cooking or eating food.

immersive
Characterized by deep absorption in something.

Indigenous
Relating to the earliest people living in a place.

mitigate
To reduce or prevent something, such as greenhouse gas emissions.

organic
A farming method that doesn't rely on synthetic pesticides, chemical fertilizers, or other artificial agents.

palate
A person's appreciation of taste and flavor.

pandemic
The outbreak of disease over a large area.

preservative
A substance added to food to keep it from spoiling.

prestigious
Having high status; inspiring respect and admiration.

rigorously
In a very thorough, detailed, and careful way.

stipulate
To demand or specify as part of an agreement or direction.

ADDITIONAL RESOURCES

SELECTED BIBLIOGRAPHY

Lincicome, Scott, and Sophia Bagley. "Food Globalization Puts the World on Your Plate." *Cato Institute*, 7 Nov. 2023, cato.org. Accessed 28 Mar. 2024.

Mariani, John. "How Immigrants from Everywhere Made American Food the Most Diverse in the World." *Forbes*, 13 Apr. 2020, forbes.com. Accessed 28 Mar. 2024.

Thiry, Marissa. "The Complexities of Ethical Eating." *Food & Nutrition*, 20 Apr. 2021, foodandnutrition.org. Accessed 28 Mar. 2024.

FURTHER READINGS

Buckey, A.W. *Land Preservation*. Abdo, 2024.

The Complete Cookbook for Teen Chefs: 70+ Teen-Tested and Teen-Approved Recipes to Cook, Eat and Share. America's Test Kitchen, 2022.

Mahoney, Ellen. *Food Stars: 15 Women Stirring Up the Food Industry*. Chicago Review, 2023.

ONLINE RESOURCES

To learn more about food and culture, please visit **abdobooklinks.com** or scan this QR code. These links are routinely monitored and updated to provide the most current information available.

MORE INFORMATION

For more information on this subject, contact or visit the following organizations:

EATER
85 Broad St.
New York, NY 10004
eater.com

Eater is a digital media brand that covers everything related to food and dining, including opinion pieces about the cultural significance of what and how people eat, articles on food fads and cooking tips, and restaurant reviews.

INSTITUTE OF CULINARY EDUCATION
Los Angeles Campus
521 E. Green St.
Pasadena, CA 91101
ice.edu/blog

The Institute of Culinary Education is the top culinary school in the United States, with locations in New York City and Los Angeles. It offers in-person and online career training and diploma, degree, and continuing-education programs in the culinary arts.

MUSEUM OF FOOD AND DRINK
55 Water St., 2nd Floor
Brooklyn, NY 11201
mofad.org

Founded by food writer David Arnold, the Museum of Food and Drink has hosted a variety of exhibits that can be tasted, smelled, and touched. Arnold and his team partner with schools and other organizations to educate people of all ages about food and its connection to culture.

SOURCE NOTES

CHAPTER 1. A CULINARY ADVENTURE

1. "Culinary Tourism Market." *Straits Research*, n.d., straitsresearch.com. Accessed 5 June 2024.

2. Willy Thuan. "6 Floating Markets around Bangkok: Which Floating Market Is Best?" *Hotels.com*, n.d., hotels.com. Accessed 5 June 2024.

3. Alexandra Domrongchai. "10 Extremely Remote Restaurants That Belong on Your Bucket List." *Food & Wine*, 10 Jan. 2023, foodandwine.com. Accessed 5 June 2024.

CHAPTER 2. GLOBAL CUISINE

1. The Kitchen Sisters. "How South Korea Uses Kimchi to Connect to the World—And Beyond." *NPR*, 22 Aug. 2016, npr.org. Accessed 5 June 2024.

2. Soutik Biswas. "The Myth of the Indian Vegetarian Nation." *BBC*, 3 Apr. 2018, bbc.com. Accessed 5 June 2024.

3. Stephanie Kramer. "Key Findings about the Religious Composition of India." *Pew Research Center*, 21 Sept. 2021, pewresearch.org. Accessed 5 June 2024.

4. "Cheese in France: Statistics and Facts." *Statista*, 18 Mar. 2024, statista.com. Accessed 20 June 2024.

5. Artem Vlasov. "Africa's Major Crop: How Climate-Smart Agriculture Is Enabling Farmers to Reap Record-High Cassava Yields Using Nuclear Science and Technology." *International Atomic Energy Agency*, 24 July 2023. iaea.org. Accessed 5 June 2024.

CHAPTER 3. THE GLOBALIZATION OF FOOD

1. Scott Lincicome and Sophia Bagley. "Food Globalization Puts the World on Your Plate." *Cato Institute*, 7 Nov. 2023, cato.org. Accessed 5 June 2024.

2. "What Countries Does McDonald's Operate In?" *McDonald's*, 21 May 2018, mcdonalds.com. Accessed 5 June 2024.

3. Lincicome and Bagley, "Food Globalization."

4. Lincicome and Bagley, "Food Globalization."

5. John Mariani. "How Immigrants from Everywhere Made American Food the Most Diverse in the World." *Forbes*, 13 Apr. 2020, forbes.com. Accessed 5 June 2024.

6. "Guns, Germs, and Steel: The Story of . . . Smallpox—And Other Deadly Eurasian Germs." *PBS*, n.d., pbs.org. Accessed 5 June 2024.

7. Aylin Woodward. "European Colonizers Killed So Many Indigenous Americans That the Planet Cooled Down, a Group of Researchers Concluded." *Business Insider*, 9 Feb. 2019, businessinsider.com. Accessed 5 June 2024.

8. Ceren Safak. "Soybeans: The Miracle Crop." *YaleGlobal Online*, 1 Mar. 2017, archiveyaleglobal.yale.edu. Accessed 5 June 2024.

9. Lincicome and Bagley, "Food Globalization."

10. Leah Bhabha. "The History of Sushi in the US." *Food52*, 29 Nov. 2013, food52.com. Accessed 5 June 2024.

11. Isaiah Reynolds. "Your Doughnut Box Is Pink Thanks to Cambodian Refugees." *Business Insider*, 10 June 2023, businessinsider.com. Accessed 5 June 2024.

12. Mariani, "Immigrants Made American Food the Most Diverse."

13. "About Najmieh." *Najmieh Batmanglij*, 2024, najmieh.com. Accessed 5 June 2024.

14. "About Najmieh."

15. Jessica Sidman. "A Star Persian Cookbook Author Opens a Destination Restaurant in Tysons." *Washingtonian*, 20 June 2023, washingtonian.com. Accessed 5 June 2024.

16. "State of the Industry: Food & Beverage Tourism in 2024." *World Food Travel Organization*, 31 Jan. 2024, worldfoodtravel.org. Accessed 5 June 2024.

17. Yetunde Oshodi-Fraudeau. "Understanding Culture through Food." *Let's Eat the World*, n.d., letseattheworld.com. Accessed 5 June 2024.

18. Lissa Poirot. "11 Biggest Food Festivals in the World, Ranked by Size." *Far and Wide*, 15 Sept. 2022, farandwide.com. Accessed 4 June 2024.

19. Oshodi-Fraudeau, "Understanding Culture."

CHAPTER 4. FOOD AND FAITH

1. Ken Chitwood. "Food's Role in Religion: Feasting, Fasting, and Faith." *Patheos*, 7 Mar. 2024, patheos.com. Accessed 6 June 2024.

2. "Jewish Practices and Customs." *Pew Research Center*, 11 May 2021, pewresearch.org. Accessed 6 June 2024.

3. Sheela Prakash. "Before and after Your Ramadan Fast: Foods for Suhoor and Iftar." *Kitchn*, 27 Feb. 2023, thekitchn.com. Accessed 6 June 2024.

4. Prakash, "Ramadan Fast."

5. Joanna Sarah-Freedman. "Ritual Eating: Food Culture from around the World." *Twisted*, 5 June 2018, twistedfood.co.uk. Accessed 6 June 2024.

CHAPTER 5. ETHICAL DIETARY CHOICES

1. Marissa Thiry. "The Complexities of Ethical Eating." *Food & Nutrition*, 20 Apr. 2021, foodandnutrition.org. Accessed 6 June 2024.

2. "The Water Footprint of Food." *FoodPrint*, 28 Feb. 2024, foodprint.org. Accessed 6 June 2024.

3. "Child Labor and Slavery in the Chocolate Industry." *Food Empowerment Project*, Jan. 2022, foodispower.org. Accessed 6 June 2024.

4. "Where We Work." *Fairtrade International*, n.d., info.fairtrade.net. Accessed 6 June 2024.

5. Thiry, "Ethical Eating."

6. "Food and Climate Change: Healthy Diets for a Healthier Planet." *United Nations*, 2022, un.org. Accessed 6 June 2024.

7. "Agriculture and Aquaculture: Food for Thought." *United States Environmental Protection Agency*, Oct. 2020, epa.gov. Accessed 6 June 2024.

8. Olivia Rosane. "'A Vicious Cycle': How Pesticide Use and Climate Change Make Each Other Worse, and What We Can Do about It." *EcoWatch*, 20 Feb. 2023, ecowatch.com. Accessed 6 June 2024.

9. "Agribusiness and Deforestation." *Greenpeace*, n.d., greenpeace.org. Accessed 5 June 2024.

10. "Organic Farming in the US—Statistics & Facts." *Statista*, 18 Dec. 2023, statista.com. Accessed 6 June 2024.

11. "Farms and Land in Farms: 2021 Summary." *US Department of Agriculture*, Feb. 2022, nass.usda.gov. Accessed 20 June 2024.

SOURCE NOTES CONTINUED

12. Jeffrey M. Jones. "In US, 4% Identify as Vegetarian, 1% as Vegan." *Gallup*, 24 Aug. 2023, news.gallup.com. Accessed 6 June 2024.

CHAPTER 6. FARM TO TABLE

1. "National Farmer's Market Week." *National Today*, n.d., nationaltoday.com. Accessed 6 June 2024.

2. "About the Farmers' Market." *Dane County Farmers' Market*, 2024, dcfm.org. Accessed 6 June 2024.

3. Mae Anderson. "Farmers Markets Thrive as Customers and Vendors Who Latched on during the Pandemic Remain Loyal." *Associated Press,* 26 June 2023, apnews.com. Accessed 6 June 2024.

4. Catie Duckworth. "Everything You Need to Know Before Signing Up for a CSA." *Tasting Table*, 14 Feb. 2023, tastingtable.com. Accessed 6 June 2024.

5. "What Is WWOOF?" *WWOOF*, n.d., wwoof.net. Accessed 6 June 2024.

6. Debbie Roos. "Community Supported Agriculture (CSA) Resource Guide for Farmers." *Growing Small Farms, North Carolina State Extension*, n.d., growingsmallfarms.ces.ncsu.edu. Accessed 6 June 2024.

7. "All about WWOOF: How It Works and What You Need to Know." *WWOOF*, n.d., wwoof.net. Accessed 6 June 2024.

8. "Farm-to-Table 256-Acre Camp and Conference Center Located in the Mountains of Julian, California." *WWOOF*, n.d., wwoofusa.org. Accessed 6 June 2024.

9. "All about WWOOF."

10. "About White Oak Pastures." *White Oak Pastures*, 2024, whiteoakpastures.com. Accessed 6 June 2024.

11. Kim Severson. "At White Oak Pastures, Grass-Fed Beef Is Only the Beginning." *New York Times*, 10 Mar. 2015, nytimes.com. Accessed 6 June 2024.

12. Alexis Burling. "How to Help the Environment: Farmers and Food Enthusiasts Have Ideas." *Washington Post*, 7 Nov. 2023, washingtonpost.com. Accessed 6 June 2024.

13. Beth Hoffman. "Op-ed: What I Learned from White Oak Pastures—And What Other Farms Can, Too." *Civil Eats*, 24 Feb. 2022, civileats.com. Accessed 6 June 2024.

CHAPTER 7. THE DINING EXPERIENCE

1. Katia Hetter. "So Much Food: Why Do Restaurants Serve Tasting Menus?" *CNN Travel*, 2 May 2018, cnn.com. Accessed 6 June 2024.

2. "Sushi Sho." *Tock*, 2024, exploretock.com. Accessed 4 June 2024.

3. "July Summer Tastings." *Bellaria*, 2024, hellariasf.com. Accessed 4 June 2024.

4. Brett Anderson. "The New Generation of Tasting Menus Won't Test Your Patience (or Your Wallet)." *New York Times*, 6 Sept. 2022, nytimes.com. Accessed 6 June 2024.

5. Jake Nevins. "Chef Charlie Mitchell Tells Us What It's Like to Get a Michelin Star." *Interview*, 8 Jan. 2024, interviewmagazine.com. Accessed 6 June 2024.

6. Charise Frazier. "Charlie Mitchell Made History as the First Black Michelin-Starred Chef in New York City—And He's Shifting the Culture in More Ways Than One." *Business Insider*, 19 Aug. 2023, businessinsider.com. Accessed 6 June 2024.

7. Katherine Boyarsky. "Food Truck Industry Trends and Statistics in 2024." *Toast*, n.d., pos.toasttab.com. Accessed 6 June 2024.

8. Boyarsky, "Food Truck Industry."

9. "Food Carts in Portland—The Story behind the Icon." *Portland by Mouth*, 20 Apr. 2020, portlandbymouth.com. Accessed 6 June 2024.

10. "14 Bucket List Culinary Experiences around the World." *Venue Report*, n.d., venuereport.com. Accessed 6 June 2024.

11. Boyarsky, "Food Truck Industry."

12. "Dining in the Dark: Seattle." *Dining in the Dark*, n.d., dininginthedarkexperience.com. Accessed 6 June 2024.

13. "Soon You Could Eat Dangling 180 Feet above Boston in Restaurant That Hoists Table for 22 Up with a Crane." *Mass Live*, 21 Feb. 2023, masslive.com. Accessed 6 June 2024.

CHAPTER 8. THE FUTURE OF FOOD CULTURE

1. "The Future of Food: What Will You Be Eating in 2050?" *HDI Global*, 14 Oct. 2021, hdi.global. Accessed 6 June 2024.

2. "Future of Food." *American Museum of Natural History*, n.d., amnh.org. Accessed 6 June 2024.

3. Jonathan Foley. "Where Will We Find Enough Food for 9 Billion?" *National Geographic Magazine*, n.d., nationalgeographic.com. Accessed 6 June 2024.

4. Foley, "Food for 9 Billion?"

5. Hannah Ritchie and Max Roser. "Half of the World's Habitable Land Is Used for Agriculture." *Our World in Data*, 16 Feb. 2024, ourworldindata.org. Accessed 6 June 2024.

6. Andrea Oyuela. "How 16 Initiatives Are Changing Urban Agriculture through Tech and Innovation." *GreenBiz*, 2 Jan. 2020, greenbiz.com. Accessed 6 June 2024.

7. Anthony Lane. "Research Green Roof Thriving at CSU Spur Campus." *Colorado State University Source*, 30 Aug. 2022, source.colostate.edu. Accessed 6 June 2024.

8. Oyuela, "Changing Urban Agriculture."

9. "The Future of Food," *HDI Global*.

10. William Brangham. "How 'Lab-Grown' Meat Is Made and Will People Accept It?" *PBS News Hour*, 27 Dec. 2023, pbs.org. Accessed 6 June 2024.

11. Danielle Wiener-Bronner. "Meat without Slaughter: Here's Everything You Need to Know about Lab-Grown Meat." *CNN Business*, 23 June 2023, cnn.com. Accessed 6 June 2024.

12. "The Future of Food," *HDI Global*.

13. Rosamond L. Naylor et al. "A 20-Year Retrospective Review of Global Aquaculture." *Nature*, vol. 591, 24 Mar. 2021, pp. 551–563, nature.com. Accessed 6 June 2024.

14. Sarah Holcomb. "The Story behind Sailors for the Sea." *Oceana*, 26 Feb. 2024, oceana.org. Accessed 6 June 2024.

15. "Future of Food," *American Museum of Natural History*.

16. Annette White. "Edible Bugs Bucket List: 25 Insects People Eat around the World." *Bucket List Journey*, n.d., bucketlistjourney.net. Accessed 6 June 2024.

17. Debbie Koenig. "The Future of Food." *WebMD*, 2 June 2022, webmd.com. Accessed 6 June 2024.

18. Bruna Alves. "Plastic Waste Worldwide: Statistics and Facts." *Statista*, 10 Jan. 2024, statista.com. Accessed 4 June 2024.

19. Paige Bennett. "Future Foods: What Will People Eat in 2050?" *EcoWatch*, 26 May 2022, ecowatch.com. Accessed 6 June 2024.

INDEX

100 Mahaseth, 8–9

Acheson, Hugh, 81
Adelaja, Angel, 91
African cuisine, 20, 22–24, 33, 58, 97
agrochemicals, 59, 62–63
American cuisine, 24–25, 26, 32–34, 80–86, 87
animal welfare, 52, 54–57, 58, 64, 65
Asian cuisine, 4, 6–7, 8–11, 16–19, 29–30, 33–34, 37–38, 50–51, 81, 84, 86, 97

Baan Tepa, 8–9
Bagley, Sophia, 28, 32
Batmanglij, Najmieh, 35
Boyarsky, Katherine, 84–85
British East India Company, 31
Buddhist traditions, 50–51

Chicago, Illinois, 4, 8, 26, 39, 54, 82
Christian traditions, 40, 48–50
Columbian Exchange, 29
Columbus, Christopher, 28
Community Supported Agriculture (CSA), 66, 71–73
culinary tourism, 6, 36–39

Dane County Farmers' Market, 70
Davis, Aaron, 99
deforestation, 63–64
Dinner in the Sky, 87

Empire State South, 80–81
environmental concerns, 52, 60–64, 88–90, 95, 97–98
ethical eating, 12, 50, 52–65
European cuisine, 19–20, 29, 30, 33, 38–39

Fairtrade, 58, 59, 65
Farm Animal Welfare Council, 55–56
farm to table, 66–77, 99
farmers markets, 66–71, 74
fish farming, 93–95
floating markets, 9
Foley, Jonathan, 88, 90
food and faith, 40–51
Food Ethics Council, 58–59
food experiences, 4, 12, 32, 39, 78, 86–87
food trucks, 38, 82, 84–86
foodie apps, 38
Fresh Direct, 91–92

globalization, 26–39
Golden, Zacchaeus, 82
Gotham Greens, 92
green roof, 91
greenhouse gas emissions, 60–62, 63, 64, 92

halal food, 45
haram food, 45
Harris, Will, 75–76
Harrison, Ruth, 55
Hindu traditions, 18, 50
Hoffman, Beth, 77

immigration, 28, 32–36
Indigenous peoples, 23–24, 31, 33
innovative farming, 90–92
insects as food, 97, 98

Jewish traditions, 33, 40–44, 50
joumou, 25

Kawafuku, 34
kimchi, 16, 17, 30
Koh Kood, Thailand, 9–10
kosher food, 42–44
Kurdieh, Zaid, 70–71

lab-grown meat, 92–93
Let's Eat the World, 37
Lincicome, Scott, 28
Little Adventures, 37
Little Tokyo, 34

Mariani, John, 30–31, 34
McLaughlin, Sue, 40
Meat Inspection Act of 1906, 55
meatpacking industry, 54–55
Mediterranean diet, 19–20, 21
Middle Eastern cuisine, 20–22
Mitchell, Charlie, 83
Muslim traditions, 7, 12, 18, 44–48, 50

New York City, 26, 70, 83, 85, 92
Ngoy, Ted, 33
No Footprints, 37–38

Oktoberfest, 38
Okuizome, 18
organic farming, 11, 58, 63, 72, 73–77, 90
Orthodox Jews, 12, 42
Oshodi-Fraudeau, Yetunde, 36–37, 39

Passover, 40–42, 44
pescatarian, 64
Portland, Oregon, 85–86

Ramadan, 45–48
Rastafarian traditions, 51
regenerative farming, 75, 76

Sarah-Freedman, Joanna, 51
seaweed, 18, 96–97
seder, 42, 44
Sha, Sarah, 98
Sharma, Asha, 63
Sinclair, Upton, 54–55
social justice, 52, 58–60, 64
Soneva Kiri, 10–11
South American cuisine, 24–25, 38
Southern Soigné, 82
street food, 8, 33–34
sushi, 18, 28, 33–34, 81, 84, 96
Sushi Sho, 81

tasting menu, 13, 78–82
Thiry, Melissa, 52–54, 59–60

vegan, 12, 64–65, 87
vegetarian, 12, 18–19, 64, 99

White Oak Pastures, 75–77
working conditions, 58–59
WWOOFing, 73–74

111

ABOUT THE AUTHOR

ALEXIS BURLING

Alexis Burling has written dozens of articles and more than 38 books for young readers on a variety of topics ranging from current events and biographies of famous people to nutrition and fitness to major milestones in history. She is also a professional book critic with reviews of adult and young adult books, author interviews, and other publishing industry–related articles published in the *New York Times*, the *Washington Post Book World*, the *San Francisco Chronicle*, and more. Alexis loves to cook—and eat—all sorts of delicious food (except insects) and lives in Washington with her husband, cats, and hundreds of books.